THE TREE
OF SOULS

KEITH FRANCIS ORGAN

The Tree of Souls

2030 East Speedway Boulevard, Suite 106
Tucson, Arizona 85719 USA
www.wheatmark.com

ISBN: 978-1-62787-616-2
LCCN: 2018942606

rev201801

Contents

ACKNOWLEDGEMENTS

To mention all the people that I met on the pathway to the Tree of Souls would be impossible. My heartfelt appreciation goes to all who held my hand when I was lost in the forest.

The first person I need to thank is my wife Shi Marie, born July 12th 1949. In our many years of marriage she's seen the good, the bad, and the ugly that comes from living with someone severely injured. Without the foundation of a good marriage, I'm certain things would have gone much worse for me. Shi's understanding gave me encouragement to endure many years of tough living conditions.

My children Shawn Lee, born December 30th, 1968 and Jennifer Marie, born, October 7th, 1971, gave us the purpose we needed to complete our circle of family life. Thank you kids for becoming loving, caring citizens that any parent would be proud of.

Tate Scott Williams, born October 4th 1999, my grandson, represents the future of our family. He is a person who exhibits great love for the peaceful beauty of the world. His excitement for what will come next on his journey restores all of our souls.

My extended family was a place where I could go for nurturing. My father, Floyd Arthur Organ, born January 15, 1912 and mother, Julia Elizabeth Connor, born December 2nd, 1914 joined together in marriage on November 15, 1934. Their love for each other produced 9 children.

Emily Ellen, born February 24th, 1935— she was the matriarch. Her bonds were very strong to the family. Emily was the sister we relied on to nurture us in times of family turmoil.

Joseph Leslie, born February 7th, 1937— he was a free spirit living his life without the restraints most of us abide by. He died very young from a heart condition. I always wonder if he sensed his early death and lived his life like there was no tomorrow.

Marion Margret, born April 3rd, 1939— of all the girls her physical and personality traits were most like our mother's.

Floyd Antinomy, born September 7th, 1941— he was the business end of the family. He loved to wheel and deal on anything. He was a great deer hunting partner over the years.

Caroline Elizabeth, born February 15th, 1944— she had a dark complexion like Dad and similar personality traits. She was a great sister to me. Carol was a very hard worker, raising two children on her own. She certainly earned my respect for living life her way.

James Ivan, born May 15th, 1946— he was a troubled soul, getting into scrapes with the law in the early days of his life. He was close in age to me, and we spent a lot of time together as children.

Irene Jeanette, born September 13th, 1950— she was a story teller who had a great imagination. She had four really great boys who meant the world to her.

Norbert Author, born September 14th, 1954— he was the warrior of the family. He almost got kicked out of kindergarten for fighting. He fathered three girls who are all tougher than I am.

Half of my siblings have gone on to be with Jesus. Their spirits are still with me. Life does not start at your birth or end at your death.

Honorable mention, a good friend, Kim Mello— we are the same age and both worked for the government during the same time period. I was always able to rap with him about what was going on in our lives, FTA.

Jim Kline, an ex-brother-in-law— he meant the world to me in my younger days. He was a person I looked to for leadership in those days after the war ended.

Mike Golozla, my prosthetist and friend— without his help I'm not sure I'd have made the walk.

Of course I need to mention men of the 9th Infantry Division. These boys had my back. I love all you guys.

FOREWORD

No one ever walks down the very same path as another. Our paths are different, depending on what life exposes us to. You may not agree with or understand my accretions, especially the healthy citizens of this country having worn rose colored glasses all their lives. They've spent their lives under a protective canopy. Hopefully, my writing will strip away some of those protective layers of lies people tell themselves. You will either hate me or love me by the time you're done reading this book.

The physical pain I dealt with after the Vietnam War has had a severe impact on the quality of my life. In my youth I thought when severe physical pain persists for long periods of time, it is joined by emotional sickness. I now understand that emotions feed sickness or wellness. It seemed like my mind was wrapped in a veil of pain. On my journey to the Tree of Souls, I've developed strategies of how to cope with life's challenges. My conclusions are based on viewing the world from a vantage point of decades of suffering.

My physical injuries from war marched in step with my emotional injuries. It was as though an entire drill team marched along in a Fourth of July parade. The cadence caller barks a command for the drill team to march in place. The emotional squad steps forward performing their drill, then seamlessly fades back into the larger group to march to their next performance site. This parade has been going on for almost 50 years for me. I recognize the members of the drill team, but to this day cannot always determine when they will perform. In times of great physical stress, they will step forth more frequently, a correlation I've learned to read.

Still there seem to be times when the rule of thumb cannot be applied. I believe it's because like the camel's back, straw has been piled on until it cannot stand one more piece.

Accumulated stress developed in my life from the fact that I could not take a break from the suffering. Didn't our Lord even have to rest on the seventh day? Unlike most human illnesses, amputations haven't any closure to them. You suffer pain daily; only the degree of suffering changes.

By prioritizing my core belief system, I was able to cope with my abnormal living conditions. What is it that actually serves me, and what is it that serves the made up needs in my life?

At times my observations were incomplete, but eventually the truth was revealed to me. I believe all people have the right to live life in a fashion that supports their basic wellness.

I sincerely hope you enjoy my journal and find my stories helpful in your journey to the Tree of Souls.

PHYSICIST ALBERT EINSTEIN

*"I know not with what weapons World War III will be
fought, but World War IV will be fought
with sticks and stones."*

ON THE MORNING OF JANUARY 20TH, 1969 I
was being loaded on a chopper heading for a field
hospital in South Vietnam.

With every heartbeat the life giving blood was pumping
from my body. I was so weak that blinking my eyes took
all the strength I had left. I felt that my death would be
coming soon and prayed that God would be waiting for me.

Searching for some way to prolong my life and control
the horrible pain, I began to hum the song "Where Have
All The Flowers Gone." The song flooded my mind until
there was no room for pain from my body. Could I keep
my body from going into shock? I'd seen men go into shock
before, and it wasn't pretty.

Any movement of my body was so painful it would tip
the song's bucket over, letting pain run back in. I'd have to
empty the pain by forcing it out of the bucket. By focusing
hard on the song, I could slowly inch my way to the top
of the bucket.

I could see bones protruding from my left leg. My right leg was also broken in several places. I tried not to look at my legs, focusing on the blades of the chopper whirling above me. I knew if this chopper didn't get me to a field hospital soon, my trip home would be in a body bag.

When the pain came it was in waves, rolling over my body like a steam roller. I was there, but my mind was not one with my body. The sound of the chopper blades seemed to come and go in the distance. I was thinking I'd never meet my son or see my wife again, that I was going to die in this damn hellhole. Then I must have been out for a while, because I was startled when the chopper landed hard on the hospital landing pad.

Emotions surfaced, and tears ran down my face. I've made it, I've made it, and will someone here please save me?

When I was pulled from the chopper I screamed, "Why don't you sons of bitches give me some morphine?" There was no reply. I wasn't sure if I'd even said it or just thought it.

I was taken into a waiting room, asked again for morphine. This time one of the nurses said, "You've already had morphine." It dawned on me that pain was not their priority. Saving my life came first.

The time it took to get my body from the chopper to the waiting room was enough time for me to regain an upper hand on the pain.

My mud-caked, bloody body was lifted from the gurney to a table. Some sort of device was fitted around my legs. I started to feel pressure on the entire lower half of my body.

I thought about screaming but instead replayed the song.

Was the device being tightened by the medical personnel pulling on strings or was I imagining things? Was I dreaming a giant blood pressure cuff was stopping the blood flow? Well, it didn't matter because for the first time I felt something was being done to save me. This old farm boy knew there was only so much blood I could lose before I'd die.

Broken bones and pieces of metal were being moved as the pressure increased, but I knew they had to stop the bleeding at any cost.

My right arm had nerve damage and my hand was in a clawed position. My fingers did not respond to commands to straighten. Blood from a small wound on my face had run into my eyes, clouding my vision. I felt like I was wetting myself but I was too embarrassed to mention it.

When the staff wasn't looking I took a look and found that some of the metal had made its way to the flag pole. Just small flesh wounds. The boys were fine. I'd had time to do an overall assessment of my body, and things looked real bad from the waist down. But the staff looked very confident and I had the feeling that injures like these were no big deal for them.

They started working on me, concentrating on controlling the bleeding. They shouted commands, grunted and exchanged looks with each other. They worked like a hill of ants, each knowing what their role was.

I lay back relaxed; my life was now in this team's hands. I'd done my job by getting myself here without going into shock.

A blood bag tainted with hepatitis C (I found that

out years later) was hung and another lifeline for fluids was added.

The staff had several small powwows. I assume that was to discuss their course of action. Like the chopper blades, they kept fading in and out. If I closed my eyes I wasn't sure if it was for a minute or an hour.

I lost track of time, and they continued to work on me. Things got quiet and someone said it was time. I was moved to another room where a nurse injected the fluid line with something and put a mask over my face.

I thought, Christ, it's about time you gave me something for pain, blur blink, blur blink, lights out.

GENERAL DOUGLAS MACARTHUR

*"The soldier above all others prays for peace,
for it is the soldier who must suffer and
bear the deepest wounds and scars of war."*

M Y BROTHER JIM AND I WOULD RAID MOM'S garden, gathering the biggest over-ripe cucumbers we could find. Then we'd take a shortcut through the pig pen to a small feeder creek that ran on our family farm. The pigs would follow us, drooling all the way to the creek, thinking the cucumbers were for them to eat. We'd give a few hollers to chase the pigs off. These hand-selected beauties had a much greater purpose than pig food.

We'd go to a place where the creek ran fast and straight for a while. The grasses had been trampled down from our previous visits. The landscape resembled a landing zone, with piles of leaves and sticks stacked up.

Dumping our T-shirts, which were folded up to hold as many cucumbers as we could get in them, we began spreading them out on the grass to select the largest ones. We cradled the cucumbers with our hands, and then lowered them into the water and watched carefully to see which side rolled up. This would establish the ship's top.

Grabbing a stick, we'd impale the cucumber to form the center pole of a ship's mast. Searching the pile of leaves we'd find the right one to make a sail. With all the parts erect, our crafts were ready for launching.

Placing our ships inline together in the fast water, we'd count to three and let go with a hard puff on the leaf. The cucumber ships would be launched. The big round cucumber sailing ships would make their way downstream to a bend where, by that time of summer, the weeds had grown up and we could no longer see them. Small ripples would misdirect their course, or sometimes they'd hit the sides of the creek and get hung up on grasses that grew from the bottom. For the ones that made that corner, we'd imagine they'd sail on to unknown destinies.

My childhood was like those small ships, following a gentle creek to larger streams, eventually ending up at the sea. There would be occasional rocks or white water rapids to safely navigate. In those times I'd draw from my family, who understood how to navigate turbulent waters. Each time this happened my emotional intelligence broadened and another pillar of support was erected to build a stronger ship.

At age 19 I joined all the rest of the ships waiting in a distant inlet harbor to be tested by the mighty sea itself. My family had done their best to build a boat that was seaworthy, but I wondered, was it ready to stand up to what the government was going to put me through?

The draft board was waiting in the open sea like a pod of killer whales patrolling the shoreline, waiting for seal pups to venture out into the deep water. The whales knew the seals had come of age, and feeding would be easy on this year's pups.

The draft board resembled the rebels in Sierra Leone, forcing poor child soldiers to do their killing. This was because we lacked the status in our society to resist.

When my draft notice came, I had three choices: play with the whales, shame myself and family by leaving our country, or go to prison.

I felt helpless and allowed the draft board to throw me into the jaws of the killer whales. Terrible storms that had been brooding for years had destroyed much better ships than mine.

I devised a plan. I'd face the storms by pointing my boat right at the waves. I had a sense that if I let the storms get me sideways I'd capsize my craft and be lost at sea.

There were many times during the storms when I felt overwhelmed. In those times I'd search for ways to keep my craft from breaking apart in the waves. In my child-hood there was my family for refuge from fear, but now I felt naked and alone. My survival skills were the only thing that could save me now.

I faced my enemies as a man ready to kill anyone I perceived as a threat. One comforting fact was that the fleet of cucumber boats fighting alongside me had the same fears. It was time for the poor child soldiers of my generation to be tested of our seaworthiness.

At this point, I thought when my war ended, I'd stop being tested, and I'd go back to life as I knew it. I wasn't aware that I'd be tested by my disability until I no longer lived on this earth.

PRESIDENT JOHN F. KENNEDY

"Mankind must put an end to war
before war puts an end to mankind"

I 'M A GRANDFATHER TO MOST OF THE MEN AND women who fought in the recent wars. My under-standing of the present generation's war is limited.

These are different times, but human suffering is a continuum. The citizens of the United States of America still order up a huge plate of suffering and the military's job is to receive or dispense the pain. I wasn't there with you in the sand, but I understand what your suffering is like. Did you ever wonder why you were the one that got caught up in the fray of this country's war? This is a question asked by everyone who became injured in a war. Did God get mad at you or what?

The answer is, God does see every sparrow that falls, but he understands that mankind must fly freely. Of course, some of us were just playing in the tide pools along the shoreline. We didn't notice the killer whales waiting for us.

Will society ever put an end to war? As long as they have the poor to sacrifice, and the rich politicians to lie about it, my guess would be no. Many Christians pray for peace, but want the military to walk them to church with an assault rifle, ready just in case God isn't listening.

Some days I believe we will continue to suffer until there aren't any more people on the planet. On days when I'm more optimistic, I feel the country will be forced into peace by our lack of ability to support future wars.

When giving thought to the situation in the Middle East, I can't see any long-term workable strategy in sight. The countries involved in the negotiations lack the maturity to think of a way to resolve the historical problems. Courageous thinkers are needed to set a new course for the Middle East.

Our returning veterans of today are in a cucumber boat, wondering how to handle a condition that they think is beyond their circle of understanding. The military puts the same armor on the outside of these little boats as they did in my day. Then they pretend they've made them into great warships, but nothing under the armor has changed.

The armor is thick enough to withstand one or two deployments in a war zone, but for some of the military, prolonged storms at sea damage their inner workings. The right way to care for any craft is to evaluate it before, during and after deployments.

The standards to get into the military needs to be raised, to satisfy the country's job description of what it takes to fight a war that lasts for generations. Maybe we could develop a robot to complement drones, which everyone really loves. It must cost fifty million dollars to kill a terrorist leader, which does nothing but prolong the war. Killing leaders is not an effective way of winning a war.

The military has gotten so good at killing sheep herders that they now are asked to train half of the world in how to kill their brothers. Aren't you proud that the United States of America educates more people in the art of killing than anyone one else in the world? I know I certainly am. Wow what a great thing to be known for.

Our country is now morphing into an ideology that drones or smart bombs will resolve our problems. Every time you drop a smart bomb to kill a few, you make enemies of many. What are we accomplishing by this bombing? If there is a fire raging, does it help to pour gas on it?

The terrorist can't hit drones by throwing a rock to strike back, so they express their anger by shooting civilians or blowing up bombs throughout the world. We appear to think if we just kill a few leaders, that will put a leaderless nation on a path to becoming a democracy.

The lack of including citizens in decisions that matter in their lives is what fuels terrorism. When there is a lack of inclusion young men turn to violence to strike back at the system that's suppressing them. You only need to look as far as this country's imprisonment of black males to validate my point.

We should allow some sort of government to form. If that government is led by someone less than perfect it will resemble ours. As time passes, we should establish diplomatic relationship with that government. Stop simplifying the process of transferring power from one dictator to another.

Transfer of power in the Middle East cannot be accomplished with our military. It simply does not work, and it's been proven many times. Governments without democratic elections, transfers the power with internal force not external force. Foreign involvement by other nations just transfers the power to the weak of that nation.

There are a bunch of wimps in Washington pretending to be men of steel. They incorrectly use the military to resolve problems. Our politicians do not understand that you do not take an elephant gun to kill a rodent, nor do you take a sling shot to kill an elephant.

When my brother Jim and I would select our cucumbers, we would gather the ones that had the best chance of completing the voyage. We knew as boys that the garden was full of cucumbers that would never make the journey.

Only highly qualified cucumbers should be in the killing business. Their handlers should be the best the country has to offer. If a soldier is found to be unfit physically or mentally to fight a war, they should be discharged from military service. The last thing this nation wants is to damage our fine young soldiers mentally or physically.

There are Americans who think all young poor people should serve in a combat zone. They're wrong; many do not have what it takes to fight in a combat zone. I'm for downsizing the military forces, only keeping the very finest our nation has to offer. Troops that could actually get something done without a mental breakdown.

The media also does a disservice to our nation's fighting men, influencing public opinion, by stereotyping wars. Nowadays movies, TV series, and documentaries zero in on the negative effects of mentally injured soldiers. What about all the troops who came back stronger and better for their military experience?

Instead of finding some balance in their work, they produce stories riddled with sensationalisms. Could they ever create a movie our troops could be proud of? These troops have been used enough by the government. Do they also have to be used by untalented small thinkers, acting like parasites, sucking the last drop of blood from our wounded soldiers?

I remember as a child watching Lassie, a child had fallen down a well. Lassie went and got help, and the child was rescued. If the writers of today were producing that series, the child would have been raped or killed in the well. The show would end with Lassie sitting on a couch having flashbacks because she couldn't save the child. When screenwriters can't produce quality work they throw in a couple of flashbacks. Kind of like someone who knows nothing about seasoning food, they taste it then search for the salt or pepper shaker.

Journalists also come up with theories of what's wrong with the troops coming back, and they publish books or articles based on those theories. I ask, does science support your stories or is it just your creative writing entertaining us?

The trouble with these stories is citizens take them as being the whole truth and nothing but the truth. Really, the journalists could be right on or they might be way off base. Talented journalists should research all sides of a story, then present an unbiased balanced report. Journalists shouldn't listen to the military too closely; they smear camouflage jelly all over the ugly parts of the war. It's been my experience that things smeared with that jelly are not good for the country.

How can it be? Only one out of every ten Sand War soldiers have a possibility of seeing any combat action. Yet 50% of the returning veterans are filing for disability due to Post Traumatic Stress Disorder (PTSD). Wouldn't you think the percentage would be more like 1% or 2%? What's going on with the military? My guess would be that 48% of them do not have PTSD.

Something else is going on in our society that we do not understand. Many are damaged when the military gets them in the first place. I'd like to tell you I know what's wrong with them, but I don't. I think part of it is the younger soldiers have some misguided sense of entitlement. These social problems are not isolated to the military. We mistakenly recognize them as sufferers of PTSD because our society loves to put labels on problems. This gives us a false reassurance of understanding.

The fact that our military is experiencing a 50% failure rate is telling a completely different story. The military is a mirror of society, representing what's happening in the civilian world. One way to solve the problem for the military is to start cherry picking from the best the country has to offer. Yes, that means if you want a career in the military you'll have to earn your way in. Once in the military you'll need to keep earning the right to stay in service. The results will be a smaller more qualified military.

Certainly, the military should embed shipwrights into the battles; they already have an excellent chaplains corps. Get some talented thinkers to assist the command group in dealing with dysfunctional, damaged troops. Give them what they need to identify the actual 1% or 2% of damaged troops in the war zones. To identify PTSD, retired commissioned officers in their fifties and sixties need to be recruited to serve as observers. They'd be the eyes and ears of the chaplain, assisting the command groups in damage control of the troops.

In Africa, poaching of large male elephants for their tusks has reduced the number of the mature bulls so much that only medium size bulls are left. On a refuge so they can be protected, reestablishment of the herd is taking place.

Biologists observing activity around a local watering hole noticed abnormal behavior. The medium size bull elephants got into a shoving contest with rhinos and killed a couple. This is not normal behavior for the mature bull elephants to kill rhinos, or for medium size bulls to exhibit that much aggression. Seems the lack of mature bulls in the herd triggered the aggression of medium size males.

The same is true with the military. They need the maturity of the senior bulls advising the young bulls of how hard to push the rhinos around.

When I think back to my own experience in Vietnam, the signs were there, but the command group did not know how to read the language of stress disorder. This would be helpful in heading off shipwrecks or at least charting maps of the sea floors to identify where the danger lies.

The establishment of parameters as to when would be the right time to remove a soldier from duty is way overdue. Damage to one's mind occurs when soldiers are kept in battle too long and they experiences too many killings.

In Vietnam, the tour of duty for the Army was one year. In recent wars, many have served in the sand for years. The reason for this is the military is now an all-volunteer organization. Without fresh meat, they keep sending the same troops back into the war zone. Should they go back to a draft? It did fuel protests of the war, which was a good thing, but definitely not. The support for fighting this country's wars will always be there. The fighting of other nation's wars is where we get into trouble.

The military, being in charge of keeping us safe, needs to focus on that mission. By doing this they think they're in the killing business. Well yes, that is the end product, but they're really in the business of physical and mental health of the soldiers. One thing I know for sure, they're not in the business of killing their own troops.

The country's model is flawed. They isolate part-time weekend warriors in war zones for extended periods of time. This ends up producing unacceptable numbers of damaged soldiers. The National Guard and Reserve Components were never meant to serve two or three tours of duty in a combat zone. I respect the heck out of them for trying, but it's just not working.

Hardened regular Army troops will be challenged to keep it together under prolonged exposure to war. Wars will always have the ability to drive a certain number of soldiers mad.

When my brother and I sailed our small crafts in the farm creek, we fitted them with sails made from leaves. Leaves were too small to catch the wind, so the ships would always follow the current downstream.

The military is not wrong to fit their ships with huge sails that force them to sail upstream. While the boats are in the military, they must follow the military wind of that God, not of their own current God.

I believe this conflict of who is the master can lead to Post Traumatic Stress Disorder. Why do most men who fight in battles weather the storms just fine? Because they understand that the government's wind really isn't a heavenly God at all; it's just a false idol made to resemble God.

You need to remember that you're isolated, brain-washed and controlled by events that represent only a very poor vantage point of the wholeness of life.

After your deployment is over, the armor on a cucumber boat is no longer needed and has to be taken off. What if there are small pieces of armor stuck on you for the rest of your life? Some scars never completely go away. Others will slowly fade as your mind learns to trust your feelings again. Scars are not all bad; they join unconnected tissue together to form a bridge for healing.

If great doctors would have been with the process from the start, they could have inserted small support pads between the armor and the skin. This would eliminate many wounds altogether and reduce the damage from others.

This process has been going on ever since we've fought wars and that's been forever. I'm sure men of past wars suffered equally, but they weren't diagnosed with any mental disorder. They laid down their weapons, rejoiced in coming back alive. They suppressed their emotions and were hugged to death by citizens grateful to have them home safe and sound.

It's an unexplainable terrible loss as to why so many young veterans today are committing suicide. My best guess is that our veterans are isolated from citizens. Troops need the full and honest support of our nation to remain healthy.

It's hard to lay one's life on the line for another's nation. The connection needs to be crystal clear for the soldiers. Wars need to belong to the country before you can win or lose them. Our military, with your support, can do the job of killing your enemies for you. Don't you think every citizen of this great nation has a responsibility to assist the military in assuring our safety? Use some common sense reasoning as to what you imagine the military can accomplish by occupying a foreign country.

The idea some veterans have of buying a gun to protect themselves against a boogieman makes absolutely no sense. You'll stand a much greater chance of killing yourself or someone you love than the boogieman. I wish someone would make an assault rifle that you loaded with flour, oatmeal, sugar and raisins. It would shoot out oatmeal cookies with an extended clip of two dozen.

When all these right-wing nuts got attacked by a bunch of kindergarten students, they could pull out their AR-15 automatic cookie assault rifle and deal with their hunger. Really, are you folks that afraid of cookie monsters that you feel the need to arm yourself with an assault rifle? Use your precious time on this earth for something other than hiding under the bed with an assault rifle locked and loaded.

Permafrost exists in the Alaskan tundra, even during the hot summer months. If you dig down a couple of feet you'll find that the ground is frozen. Today our country has established a permawar so even during the short time periods between wars, elected officials are frozen in the war mode.

The permawar plan goes something like this: We invade a foreign country and dismantle the current government. We then spend billions of dollars to install a new puppet democratic form of government. This total dismantling of other nation's governments leaves huge voids in the leadership. Those voids are then filled by extremists. What is the military to do with them? The balance of power for the whole region is upset, and the lunatics are running the nut house.

If you look at what the military accomplished in a short window of time, you might get the idea that the whole operation was successful. On further examination of our involvement in changing other nation's governing bodies, we'd find a total disaster for our foreign policy and for the people we are trying to help.

We cannot do it with might. Change will have to be accomplished over time by shining a light on areas that can be illuminated when opportunities avail themselves.

4

REVEREND MARTIN LUTHER KING JR.

"Wars are poor chisels for carving out peaceful tomorrows."

WASHINGTON D.C. HAS BEEN BLINDED BY being in the darkness too long. It's time to transplant new eyes into our nation's governing body that can see clearly into the future. The country must come to an understanding that the military shouldn't fight endless wars.

They also need to develop new methods of dealing with damaged soldiers. No matter what kind of action you've seen, when all the fighting is over, the veterans need to explore the small streams of their youth. When they come to a place where the water is still, the images of their emotions will appear.

When you see that huge metal sail the military puts on you, reach up, take it off. Replace the metal sail with a sail made of leaves. Oops you say, the metal sails are stuck on too tight and you can't dismantle them. That comes from too much isolation in the made-up environment of war, so it may take more than one attempt to soften your sails to operate in the real world.

At this point don't lie to yourself and mask over the images with drugs, boozes or living in denial. You have to lay down the sword of hatred that the government loaned you. Commit your life's purpose to honor your true self. It's the time to explore ways of building a good life that fulfills the basic needs of all people. Which is love of family, meaning of your existence, and service to others.

There is a time for war and a time for peace, not only on a personal level but also on a national level.

In Vietnam, our country's leaders whipped up the fear of communism taking over the world. In the Middle East it was weapons of mass destruction. Neither proved to be a credible threat to our national security. The soldiers who fought both wars did their best to make our nation safe. We were used and lied to by leaders we thought were honest, informed thinkers.

That doesn't make your sacrifice any less, because all soldiers of any war are doing their best to protect our nation. We must guard against the folks who would like to hurt us, but not be sucked into wars by half-truths.

Our leaders keep changing, so they have to learn what stick to take to the woodshed. Should they take a really big one and shock and awe them or maybe take a little stick and threaten to use it?

Resolution of difficult problems is a continuum spanning over many president's terms. Policy needs to be well-reasoned and followed no matter what flavor of the month is running Washington. The correct time to fight a war is when the ruling party is proposing to start one.

In wars that we are not in immediate danger, the public

should have to vote on it before committing resources. The ruling party would have to present a timeline for completion, what its goals are and how they expect to achieve them.

If they get approval from the citizens, they'd next have to seek approval from the United Nations. But isn't that too complicated, involving all those people? Yes, you've got it. The idea of committing troops to war needs to be done correctly.

One day after Brother Jim and I had become grown men, we were out fishing in a small boat. He said, "You know, every scar I have on my body came from you."

I said, "No way."

Then he pointed out the time I ran into him with a sled and cut open his ankle and pulled down his sock to show me. He continued, "And then there was the time when we got into a fight in the milk house and you broke a cup and then cut my shoulder."

"Well yes," I said, "but that was an accident and I got the belt from Dad for my temper."

"Then the time when we were horse playing on ice and I fell and cut my knee open."

I said, "Okay I give up. I did give you a few scars, but you'd look like some kind of sissy without them. I also was your little brother and it took me a long time to earn your respect."

With that remark we broke into laughter. My brother's scars came from me.

This country's scars came from cutting ourselves with the sword of revenge that a few extremists provided us. Washington grabbed the sword and stuck it in both our eyes and we went blind from rage. After a certain amount of time, that revenge became self-inflicted sickness, doing harm to whoever continues to carry it in their heart.

My brother Jim had the need to show me the scars I had given him. I had the responsibility to acknowledge my part in him getting them. Why did he forgive me for giving him those scars? Because our brotherly love for each other was far greater than a few scars.

Is it possible for this country to sit by the reflecting pool with our returning soldiers? For all of us to take ownership of our responsibilities to protect our country? To honor their service by including them in a conversation of how we can thaw out the permawar that exists in our country? Start a new conversation of peace with our enemies?

There is a river of tears flowing for the loved ones lost over the years in all of America's Wars. They have stained our lands and cut deep divisions in the landscape. These great seeping springs of tears are stored in the tear ducts, ready for tomorrow's children.

There has to be a way to stop the flow of tears. Certainly, if we traced the history of our involvement in the Middle East back in time, we could adjust our foreign policy to consider the best course of action to follow. One would have to study history to evaluate the reasons so many states are failing in that region. My guess is that the trouble grew as the wealth of the planet became too concentrated. This set the stage for wars, migration of people and hatred of the grain keepers.

The growing number of citizens in this country who feel left out of the main stream is also evident to anyone who has their eyes open. The rich will push the poor of the country down until they rise up. You see it in the general elections of today—candidates cherry picking solutions to complex problems. It's easy to claim to have the answers to a few of the over-ripe cherries. What to do about a whole orchard of spoiling cherries is another question. Our cowboy mentally hasn't helped in my opinion.

When my son was around four years old he announced that he didn't like his name Shawn.

I asked, "Is there another name you like better?"

"Yes, I like the name Billy. Could you call me that from now on?"

"Well, we certainly can," I replied. "And you know, the name Billy reminds me of a cowboy I used to know."

So for a couple of weeks we had a full-blown cowboy in the house roping, riding, and chasing down outlaws.

Jennifer, little sister Princess Smelly Pants, whom I believe came from the Running Bare tribe, had to play the part of the renegade Indians in the area.

I was deputized to assist in chasing down outlaws.

Mom would help Smelly Pants hide. Then, on a mysterious sign, Smelly Pants would launch a surprise attack on the settlers.

It wasn't long before Jennifer protested of always being the outlaw and wanted to be on the good guy's team.

So, Mom sat down with the sheriff and together they came up with a plan to allow the Running Bare tribe to take turns being the good guys once in a while.

The sheriff didn't really like this arrangement, but he knew Smelly Pants had Mom in her corner, so he went along with the new plan.

It wasn't too long after that agreement, the sheriff quit his job. Seems it wasn't as much fun getting roughed up by little sister and mean Mom.

The next thing we saw was the retired sheriff with a cape flying around the house playing Superman.

All over the world too much power is so concentrated in a few people's hands. Common folks can't even dream of receiving a fair shake in their lives.

Will the folks in Washington ever understand that we shouldn't try to rope, tie-up and brand the children of the Middle East with our cowboys? Our nation needs to foster other countries while they're going through their cowboy stage of life. Hopefully some of the greedy will allow those countries to share in the earth's harvest and they will no longer need to ride the war horse.

Nations have belief systems supported by years of traditions. Those traditions follow generations of believers and become social norms. It can take generations to change thinking, or just a few leaders to change people's thinking for the good or bad.

There are many things we can do to help the poor people in the world. For one, sharing the earth's resources with them would be a start. Forcing a democracy onto people whose basic living conditions do not support advanced forms of government isn't going to work. I believe that poverty is the root cause of the Middle Eastern wars.

In the Middle East, there is very little space for the introduction of balancing principals. Either you conform or it's off with your head. Our country also has the off-with-your-head folks and occasionally they come to power, but eventually retire to Texas.

To bring our country back into balance, we find some liberal from a place like Arkansas with honey dripping off her lips. Her agenda is to solve all the world's problems with government funding and thinks no one should take any responsibility for their own life. Of course, neither type of extremist is right, but over time they balance each other out.

Most of our politicians do not appreciate that the opposing view is critical to running a country correctly. The founding fathers knew that these two sides needed to come together with open minds and discuss the challenges that are common to all people. Both sides have to agree to consider each other to have equal status at the table. Well, at least they used to.

I'm certain that the Middle East has great leaders that know what I'm saying is the truth. So when you setup your government, don't make it like ours is today. Make it like ours used to be when it was formed. Now, that I have straightened out the Middle East, I'll get back to grief consulting.

If you're a poor boy like me who got caught up in a war and you're having trouble grieving the loss of a friend, come sit a while. Grandpa needs to share this story with you.

Our daughter, Jennifer, became pregnant and shared the news with us. This was our first grandchild and we could hardly contain our happiness. All through the pregnancy, all of us kept busy getting everything ready for the blessed event. The baby was due in a few days.

We received a call from my daughter and she was concerned that the baby wasn't moving much. The same day, I had to go into Madison Veteran's Hospital for some serious back problems. A couple of days later my wife called and told me the baby had died and a still born birth was scheduled. When I returned home my wife and I went to the hospital to give our daughter and our son-in-law support.

Our beautiful granddaughter was delivered and the nursing staff prepared her for us to hold. When the baby was put into my arms, I could hardly maintain my self-control. I didn't want to upset our daughter, so I tried my best not to break down.

I kept thinking, why would God allow the cord to wrap around her neck and kill her? What did this little girl do to deserve an ending like this? Maybe God is paying me back for something I did in this lifetime.

The outside was calm, but my heart was being broken into small pieces. I felt unconnected with my emotions, sort of in a state of numbness.

In a few days we had a private funeral. I thought this broken heart would mend itself back together after the activity of events was over. The first week after the burial, when I was alone, I had a breakdown. The pain was so raw it cut me like a razor slicing away at my heart.

I thought, This is just the first week, things will get better. They did improve, but it took months to finally be able to speak to others about my loss.

My wife wasn't any better. A month later, a baby was being baptized in church and she broke down and left church early. Even to this day if you catch us on the wrong day we can tear up about our lost first grandchild.

Like most people, I've lost family and friends who were dear to me for many years. So why did I have such a great sense of loss for my granddaughter whom I had never met?

I believe it had something to do with the events leading up to her death. I was so looking forward to her birth. When she was snatched from us at the last minute, my mind couldn't make any sense of it.

I share this story with you in an effort to reveal the

connections the returning veterans have to explore to understand the grieving process.

The pain comes from things beyond the death of your friends. Its roots reach back into the unit's relationship with each other. Did you have high expectations that everyone was coming home alive together? Maybe you thought if everyone did their job correctly you'd all make it home because you're each other's brothers. You had set yourself up for a walk on the denial side of life.

You had turned on all the artificial lighting you could find. Then the unthinkable happened and your good bud was killed and you were left in the darkness.

You understand the concept of night vision. In the evening around sunset all artificial light is turned off. Your eyes slowly adjust to the available sunlight. When it's completely dark, you can see much better than if you had left the lights on and suddenly shut them off.

For nine months before our granddaughter was born, I was turning on every emotional light in my mind. When the darkness came, I couldn't see, and it took some time for my mind to adjust to the available light.

If you explore those connections, you should arrive at a point where balance can be restored to the emotional damage you've experienced. If you own the darkness, it becomes like the light and you can achieve balance of your emotions. At first, balance is difficult, but with persistence you will master the art of night vision.

If you look for all the answers too soon, you will not be able to see them. Give yourself enough time for the pupils of your eyes to dilate. Every day at sunset you have a new opportunity to reset your night vision.

5

GENERAL ROBERT E. LEE

*"It is well that war is so terrible,
otherwise we should grow too fond of it."*

I GREW UP ON A DAIRY FARM IN WESTERN Wisconsin. I understood at a young age our family's relationship with killing domestic livestock and what ended up on the table for supper.

We were also a hunting family, harvesting the bounty of the wild. Killing of livestock and wild game seemed natural to me. If mom had us chopping off chicken's heads, we knew there'd be chicken on the table on Sunday.

We butchered in the fall in those days, which meant we killed pigs or maybe a beef cow for ourselves. We never enjoyed the killing. There was an unspoken understanding that the animal should be killed with the least amount of suffering possible. We were taught from the crib that this was the way rural people survived.

When we lived on the farm, lots of people from town mistakenly assumed we had room for all their unwanted cats. They'd drop them off for us to care for. Pretty soon, we would have 30 cats. We did need 5 or 6 cats to keep the rats and mice from over running the place, but not 30. Then if we didn't do something about it, pretty soon, we'd have 200 cats. So, the day would come when Dad would bring out the rifle to shoot cats until he reached the carrying capacity of the farm.

Stray dogs were another problem we had. They'd show up, kill one of our calves or get into the hen house to kill chickens. Once again Dad would bring out the rifle to shoot the dog. We didn't enjoy killing cats or dogs, but what was a struggling farm family to do with other people's unwanted pets?

The Catholic faith taught us that men were dominant over the animals on Earth and it was right to harvest them for our consumption. They placed man above the rest of the earth's inhabitants. We are God's favorite.

Today I'd have a hard time shooting a dog or cat. I still hunt deer, but if I watch the animal too long I have a hard time shooting it. My understanding of man's connection to Mother Earth's inhabitants has softened. In my golden years I now give all God's creatures more respect.

As a child, killing another person was unthinkable. We were taught to love our fellow man that taking a human life was a sin, even an unborn baby. As a matter of fact, it was one of the Ten Commandments.

These distinctions were very clear, and they made sense as long as I operated on that playing field.

At age 19, I was out of high school, earning a living working in a factory. I'd met the girl of my dreams, and we were about to get married when my draft notice came in the mail. We went ahead with the wedding and had a short honeymoon.

Three days later I was on my way to Fort Campbell,

Kentucky to begin my education in how to kill communist people.

A few days later my official basic training started, I was sitting in a day room when this nasty little man with a smoky the bear hat on came to collect us. He started screaming, calling us dirty names, telling us he didn't understand how he always got stuck with the screw ups.

He informed us that he didn't care if we sent letters to our congressmen; he used those for butt wipes. When addressing him we should always scream "Yes, drill sergeant!" and "No, drill sergeant!"

Then he said, "From now on, when you sit down you will scream the words, *Vietnam! Kill the Cong! Infantry!*" That was until you're out of basic training.

Wow, I thought, this guy has a problem. After thinking about it for a couple of weeks, I realized this was his way of brainwashing our minds, hardening our hearts to hate this country's enemy. He needed to get these lambs ready for the slaughter of those little yellow people. In a few short months, he had to teach young boys to hate people they had never met.

The drill sergeant's first job was to challenge all those ideas your priest, father, mother, and teachers had put in your head. This was done by reducing our sense of self-worth, making us feel we were the lowest snake that crawled on earth. I and all the rest of the guys hadn't realized that, until we met him, our thinking was flawed.

Once he had reduced us to a state of feeling like worthless, wimpy momma's boys, a new man could be born from the ashes. Now, we were his men from his great company. Having feelings of respect for human life was incorrect thinking. If we wanted to make him proud and honor the United States Army, we'd have to start thinking like him, a real man. A few of us at the time understood the implications of all this B.S. but we realized we would be wise to play along.

Another thing he did was to always call enemy soldiers by some made-up name like Gooks, Charlie, or Yellow Bastards. This was his way of making them something less than human. If you could think of them as less than human—not as sons, fathers, husbands, or part of the human race—it would be a lot easier to kill them.

Of course, the drill sergeant knew what we were in for, and he was doing his best to keep us from coming home in a body bag. The brainwashing went on for a couple of months, and it was kind of working. Certainly, the young men were getting the idea, becoming much more aggressive.

The brainwashing also included lots of physical training, which increased the physical fitness of the men. We felt a lot tougher the day we graduated from basic training than the day we started. In eight weeks, I had been transformed from a momma's boy into one of the drill sergeant's lean mean fighting machines.

From Fort Campbell, I was sent to Fort Lewis, Washington to complete Advanced Infantry Training.

When I got there, the drill sergeant was similar. We were a *little* better than the lowest snake that crawled the earth, *but not a lot*. He also did not understand why he always got the screw ups, but would see if he could build us up into real men that he could be proud of.

Much of the training was similar too, with more detail given to weapons training and survival skills. They introduced additional brainwashing methods, relying on rewards or insults to get the job done.

In the military, things like uniforms, medals, and ribbons are used to set one apart from the general crowd. As your time in service increases so does your rank, and everybody is very aware of the pecking order. You'll make rank easier if you're a front line dog, and medals will be showered on you.

In Advanced Infantry Training you're first insulted. Then praise starts to increase as you draw nearer to graduation. So it's a little less crap every day.

The command group took the weekends off. They'd have some wannabe drill sergeants take command. On one Sunday, a wannabe sergeant was getting in the face of a man in formation when all of a sudden, the kid hauled off and knocked the wannabe on his butt. I believe that was the last time they had wannabes take temporary command of the soldiers. Men in that formation had been brainwashed by hardened senior drill sergeants. We knew you needed to be the real deal to take command.

In a few weeks, I graduated from Advanced Infantry Training. I was about to be shipped to Vietnam when my dad had a heart attack. The Army gave me a compassionate duty assignment for a month before shipping me to Vietnam. The break was not a good thing, because when I was deployed to Vietnam, some of the meanness had worn off. I wondered if I had enough hate in my heart to kill the Cong.

I was stationed with the 9th Infantry division, a mean, lean outfit. The army was losing lots of men at that time, so I was deployed by myself. I remember thinking it would have been better to have deployed as a unit, but after the troubles the Iraq and Afghan vets are having, I've rethought it. I believe it's harder to lose a brother than a stranger, so maybe I was lucky not to be too close to others in my unit.

Our job was to kill as many of the Viet Cong as possible. Washington wanted a large body count. It was our job to make them look good, so we were to keep slaughtering those poor boys off. They needed to show the voters that things were going as planned.

I know lots of people in this country were beginning to have their doubts about the war, but Washington had to put on a good front. The public just didn't understand. Surely the politicians thought if we could kill enough Cong, we would deliver a victory for the country, which would make everything right.

It also didn't hurt that most of the American lives being lost were poor people's kids who didn't really matter because of their standing in the class system that exists in this country. After all, the rich folks got their kids deferments. So what if 58,209 mostly poor kids died? This country officially abolished slavery on January 31, 1865, but really drafting poor kids into the military to fight another country's civil war was a form of slavery.

What was I talking about before I got side tracked beating up rich folks? Oh I remember, my first couple of operations in the field, nothing really happened. We patrolled for three days and then went back to base camp for a day. Base camp was just tents, bunkers, with razor wire strung around the perimeter. We picked up our mail, wrote some letters, took a shower in dirty water from a canal, and then grabbed a couple of hot meals.

The guys might play a little ball if someone could come up with a ball. Whatever ball they came up with was the game we played. Mostly we just rested, sat around listening to Marvin Gaye singing "I Heard It Through the Grape Vine." Or once in a while they'd play, "Detroit City (I Wanna Go Home)" by Bobby Bare. That always got a lot of attention. Then back to the field for more slogging through the rice paddies with wet clothing for three days.

The mosquitoes would eat you alive if you didn't have a poncho liner that they couldn't drill through. Then of course, everyone's favorite, the leeches and snakes were waiting for you in the water. Or you'd walk under a low hanging branch and 100 fire ants would fall down the back of your neck. On most days the temps would be above 90 and very humid, so you were always miserable.

They fertilized the rice paddies with human waste or whatever came out of the south end of a north facing water buffalo. The whole country had a stench to it. The water buffalo didn't care for the smell of American soldiers. It must have been the smell of soap that upset their sensitivities.

It was like taking a trip back in time. Everything was done with water buffaloes, wooden plows and human labor. The poverty was everywhere, people half-starved to death, eating dogs to stay alive. If someone in the family got sick they just died. There weren't any doctors available for rural farm people. This place was the worst place I could image on this planet.

Once in a while we'd get easy duty, clearing a road for the Engineers or guarding a bridge. We usually could talk a mama san into cooking us some rice with fish or duck. After a couple of weeks of eating C-rations, you'd do anything for fresh cooked food.

Mostly it was a very boring existence, except for when we saw action. Someone would step on a booby trap or a firefight would erupt from the thick jungle. We would lose a couple of people mostly to booby traps, and then go back to miserable living conditions.

Once the injured guys were on the medivac chopper heading for the field hospital, we'd stand around and discuss if they'd be back or would be going home. The longer I was there the meaner and harder I became.

As the injuries occurred more frequently, the morale of the men started showing the effects. I remember one day after an exhausting march across a rice paddy, we came to a road. The men needed to let off some steam and were in a playful mood. Some South Vietnamese civilians were riding by on motor bikes.

The guys started throwing some smoke grenades on the back of the bikes in a friendly manner. Then some Vietnamese took offense and raised their fists in a threating manner. It turned from a playful exchange, to deadly serious in a second.

I really thought civilians were going to get killed before it was over. Finally the squad leader defused the situation with a few words. That's why you always need a good handler when the pit bulls are tasting blood and would like nothing better than to go for the throat. The dogs were at the end of their emotional chains, and biting anything that was thrown at them seemed justified.

After spending time in the field as a front line dog, you truly need to adjust to the brutalities of killing. This wearing down of a soldier's internal checks and balances is the reason things can get out of hand. Some event can set off the men on a rampage that without good leadership will get out of hand. For that reason you shouldn't judge the military from your reclining chair with a puppy sitting on your lap.

In 1968, there were two or three major offensives by North Vietnam. The 9th Infantry was in the delta, with Charlie streaming down from the north. Only two things to do, kill or be killed.

Most of the intelligence we received didn't pan out, they had us chasing around a herd of water buffalo thinking it was an enemy encampment. I always thought the pecking order was human intelligence, animal intelligence, and last of all military intelligence.

Then one day it was for real. We had gotten in close to the regular NVA unit, and they were flushing out of the thick jungle cover like a covey of quail. It was payback time for all the men we had lost at their hands. Even the old man had his chopper out spraying the jungle with machine gun fire to help flush them out.

I saw movement out of the corner of my eye. I turned to see a North Vietnamese Regular coming right at me. I raised my M-79 and let him have a canister round. It took him off his feet and at the same time blowing up an enormous bee hive.

The whole area was filled with the biggest bumble bees I've ever seen. One of the guys asked if he could retrieve the weapon. I thought that was odd, like it was my kill and I had some say so in who was allowed to pick the corpse first for souvenirs.

I said, "Go for it. We can trade it for some good food," which grunts had a hard time getting. Souvenirs didn't mean a thing to me, but guys that didn't see any action got off on all that crap.

I stayed put, avoiding close observation of the corpse. I didn't want the image of his face burned into my memory for the rest of my life. The guy who went to retrieve the weapon was just about to pick it up when bees started stinging him.

He began slapping the bees, which did nothing but stir up the hive more. He then ran and jumped into a small creek not deep enough to cover his body. It was getting down right entertaining. Then he came out of the water running, putting some distance between him and the hive. That did work, but by that time he was covered with bee stings.

Gun fire erupted from not more than 100 meters away and our attention shifted to address it. The whole battle went on for maybe a half-hour, and I was proud of the way our guys fought. After things quieted down, the bee keeper's face had swollen up so much he could hardly see.

I was awarded a Bronze Star, yet I felt I didn't deserve such an honorable medal. I thought, Why not give it to one of those regular army boys hiding out in a non-combat M.O.S. Think of the attention they'd get telling stories at the veterans' hospital. Of course it was the Army's way of encouraging me to kill more of them. No need to waste a Bronze Star on this grunt. I was glad to do the killing. I thought, At least this son of a bitch wouldn't be setting a booby trap to kill one of our guys tomorrow.

So, what had happened to the momma's boy from Wisconsin? Was I totally sick? Was it the right thing to do? Well, yes, I was a little sick of being on the receiving end of what they were handing out. I acted out of self-interest. I didn't want to go home in a body bag or see my buddies wounded. So why not send this yellow bastard to meet his maker?

I believe before I entered the service, I had been shielded from the dark side of human behavior. I had made the correct adjustment to do what my country was asking of me. In my younger years, mom and dad had placed soft filters in my field of vision to allow my humanity to surface. What the war did was strip away my humanity, replacing it with a need to survive. I was there to act as the executioner for the army.

I'd finally gotten into the right frame of mind. My humanity was driven far below the surface. I wondered. Would my mind ever regain the pure innocence of my youth? That's a privilege reserved for few in a war. This operation brought my mind to an awakening. I now had walked in the shadow of death, seeing what was down in that dark valley.

That day defined my parameters. From that point on, I knew that killing was something that I had to do. To hell with what the priest, teachers, or my parents had taught me as a child. They were living in denial, not recognizing evil is a brother to love. After that day, if my unit lost a few men, I'd be okay. It was the new norm for me. I guarded myself from getting too close to the guys because I needed that emotional distance to remain sane.

I had one really good bud named Roy who was like a brother to me. I shared my fears with no one else, and I didn't have to worry about what I said to him. We did our very best to watch out for each other. I remember playing "what if" with him. What would be the worst thing that could happen to us?

Being captured by the yellow bastards would be the worst or getting hit in the head and coming back a vegetable, or maybe becoming blind. Well, not too long after that conversation I found out. We were out on patrol, a booby trapped 105 artillery round exploded and three of us were hit. No one was killed, but there were some serious injuries.

I was sent to a field hospital where they performed a left leg amputation, cast my broken right leg, and wire-stitched my wounds closed. So just when I was ready to do some serious killing for my country, I had to reevaluate my standard operating procedures. The lean mean fighting machine had come to an end. There would be no more killing for me. It was time for me to begin the process of healing my body and mind.

Will I Be The Tiger or the Prey?

Two furious tigers patrol these killing pastures.
Oh, where does tiger live today?
Blood from previous kills stains my memories.
Will I be the tiger or the prey?

I sense we will meet today.
Carefully I investigate his familiar hiding places.
Step, look, pray, tiger are you here?
Will I be the tiger or the prey?

I am tiger, or is he tiger?
Claws will injure, teeth will kill.
I sense tiger is near.
Will I be the tiger or the prey?

Tiger's snare hurls me skyward.
I feel his claws sink into my flesh.
Will tiger's teeth kill me today?
For today I'm the prey.

6

SENATOR JOHN F. KERRY

"I saw courage both in the Vietnam War and in the struggle to stop it. I learned that patriotism includes protest, not just military service."

I REMEMBER WAKING UP IN THE HOSPITAL AND looking down to see that my left leg was missing. I was so full of morphine that my mind could not process the loss of my leg.

An army nurse reached into my small morphine bubble, taking my hand. I hadn't noticed her until she touched me with her lovely warm hands. She spoke in a soft comforting tone, reassuring me that I was in her care.

My emotions welled up in me. I felt like crying, yet I didn't understand why. The loss of my leg did not really fully register in my mind, so what was causing my emotions to surface?

It was the fact that another human had spoken softly, touching me in a gentle way. This action unlocked the emotional door that had been closed by the brutality of the war. The caring concern streamed from the nurse's hands.

At first my mind was shaken by the unfamiliar sensation of the touch of another human. I could not find any words to express my feelings. I eventually recovered my composure and said, "Thank you for caring." I did my best not to show any emotions. My tears were shed in my mind, not in my eyes where she would see. Grunts, after all, don't cry in front of nurses. Do they?

The war was fresh in my mind and I couldn't figure out which master to serve. Should I hold on to the ugliest part of human behavior, or was it okay to allow this nurse's caring manner to release some of the suppressed emotions?

She let go of my hand, which lessened the intensity of the experience. Her touch was a powerful tool she used to show her level of commitment to the guys waking up with some serious injuries. Nurses are such lovely people. They gave so much to the returning Vietnam veterans. She had started the process of reinstalling the humanity that I had suppressed during my tour of duty. I can't even remember her face, but her hands were of an angel.

I spent another couple of weeks in the field hospital in Vietnam before gaining enough strength to be transferred to Japan. I remember being wheeled down the hall of the army hospital on a gurney. It was an open bay, with pull curtains between each soldier. It smelled like a slaughter house, and everywhere I looked there was another guy with amputated legs or arms.

So I said to the orderly pushing me, "Does it always smell like this in here?"

To that he replied, "Be thankful you're not in the burn ward."

By the time I got to my bed I was sick from the smell of rotting flesh. It was hard to look at all those guys suffering and not come away from it humbled, appreciative of not having more wrong with me.

I stayed in Japan sicker than a dog for a month. Finally I was shipped to Fitzsimons Army Hospital in Denver, Colorado. There my doctors were trying to figure out a way to save the other leg. The leg had thirteen breaks in the bone from the knee to the ankle, allowing a bone infection to develop. Every day they'd stick a large needle into my leg, just below my knee and push a pint of green puss out a hole above my ankle.

This treatment plan had been going on for around a month and things weren't getting any better. My spirits were down, and I was suffering from depression. I was unable to clearly focus on what would come next in my life.

When my family came down, my wife was told, "We are trying to save his leg." My wife, Shi and her mother took my son Shawn out of the room for some reason. My mother was alone in the room with me.

Mother could always sense when I was hurting. Speaking softly, Mom said, "Honey, you'll have lots of struggles in your life with your disability. Don't worry. Over time, your mind will reveal to you what your heart already understands. You have an Irish heart, which will lead you out of your depression.

"In my life I've known many people who have a much greater disability than yours. There are two types of intelligence: intellectual intelligence, which serves a small part of your needs, and emotional intelligence, which serves every other need you have.

"These folks didn't realize that their hearts need to rule them, not their minds. Your Irish heart is fully developed. It will allow you to move beyond what is torturing you."

I got it right away. Mother had reassured me in only a few sentences that my humanity would reappear. Mother knew where the pain was and what medicine was needed to help. She told me that my childhood was tough, but that gave me the strength I would need to survive. I had all the necessary skills to cope with any condition life would give me.

I remember saying, "Mom, it didn't give me the skills to deal with the yellow bastards."

She looked straight into my eyes. "I'll give you temporary permission to hate your enemies. Give yourself time to grieve properly. Then let you're Irish heart replace the hatred with the original plan God had for you. I didn't raise you to judge people by their color. Do you realize Saints also come in yellow?"

Then she said something I'll never forget. "You run the risk of becoming what you hate, a white bastard."

Of course, Mom was right. A person's color means nothing, and we have certainly allowed color to separate us way too long.

She continued. "Give the hatred of the yellow race back to the United States of America. After all, that's where it came from. *Don't personalize the war.* Hatred's power comes from you holding on to it. You need to control your thoughts from the inside out, not let others control you from the outside in.

"You have to recognize the fact that hatred of the North Vietnamese doesn't belong to you. You were only brainwashed into thinking that you hated the color yellow."

I replied, "It's hard to love someone when they're trying to kill you."

Mom then brought up the Second World War. She recalled during the war everyone in this country hated the Germans and the Japanese. "After the war, the country forgave our enemies and now they are our friends. The only people I know that are still tormented by their hatred of Germans or Japanese are the bitter old men that I take care of in the nursing home."

Mom was deeply concerned about my feelings of hatred toward a whole race of people. She seldom let her feelings show, but she began to cry uncontrollably. It seemed she cried enough tears for all the grieving mothers whose children came home injured or in a body bag.

I kissed Mom on the cheek and told her I would call my enemies Charlie from now on. "Charlie, what's the meaning?" She asked. "Mom, it's a military phonetic alphabet. North Vietnamese Communist (NVC) is November Victor Charlie. That's a mouthful, so it ended up just Charlie."

"Okay, that will be alright," she said.

I was hoping to give her some emotional stability for a few minutes so she could stop sobbing. I think Mom recognized at that moment what emotional damage had been done to me. She knew the physical disability was manageable, but emotional injuries could destroy me without leaving one visible mark.

PTSD was an injury that would affect many of the young men's humanity coming back from the war. After a few more minutes of crying, her pain seemed to lessen and her tears stopped flowing. She sat quietly. I could tell she was searching for the best way to verbalize her plan to help me heal my emotional wounds.

She began by recalling the days of my growing up on the farm, how life made sense to both of us. We talked about how the whippoorwills would sing us to sleep with their songs in the late summer evenings. We spoke of watching for the first arrival of blue birds in spring. Dad said the males came first to stake out their territories. And we talked about the times when frogs would get into our pipes from our spring and we'd spend hours getting them out.

She continued to call up old memories of when my humanity was formed by her. She was trying to make the point that the war's effects would fade. I'd come back to her, back to the gently loving person Mom had sent to Vietnam.

She was sure my emotions had been contaminated by the virus of war. Like most viruses, the body overcomes them in time with chicken soup and rest. Mom was making the point that the killing I did for this country was not who I was, that actually I was a gentle momma's boy.

For a couple of hours we concentrated on the innocent times before this government abused so many poor American families. I knew that mom felt betrayed by her country for continuing this senseless slaughter of young men. She said this would never have happened if John Kennedy had lived. He was right under the pope to her.

Then she recalled the time in Irish history when people starved because the potato crop had failed. The fact that poor Irish people were starving didn't matter to the English. Many migrated to this country during that time. When they got here, they were treated badly by Americans.

So the Irish have always been abused by the self-appointed elitists of the world. For many years the Irishmen put up with the abuse of the elitists. Then one day, the Irish Republican Army was formed.

Mom quickly said, "I never believed in violent actions,

but for those Irish it was their way of sending a message to the government."

I asked, "So if the draft dodgers didn't go to war because they were afraid to fight, is that wrong?"

Mom said, "Yes that would be wrong."

"But if they didn't go to war because they love their country and wanted to send a message to the government, they were right?"

"Yes, that's right," Mom said. She started to cry again. It was the government's fault these young men were forced to make terrible decisions that would affect their whole life. She said the government had been fighting a war without the blessings of the citizens for way too long. She said, "The damn government has lost its credibility to lead our nation."

Mother said "damn," which wasn't a word she used, and I noticed a drop in her voice when she said it.

I dropped the discussion immediately. I didn't want to cause more pain for her. I wasn't far enough along in my healing process to understand what she was telling me.

My wife and mother-in-law popped their heads into the hospital door with baby Shawn, and our conversation came to an end.

They had news that a big snowstorm was about to hit and they would have to fly home. Mom gave me a concerned look, because I'm certain this was her first flight on a plane. Old man winter did let loose with a darn good snowstorm.

After making arrangements, the family returned to Wisconsin. It was certainly great to see my wife. Shi looked great, but under the surface I could tell she was troubled. Holding my son for the first time seemed to complete a connection between a father and son that you don't get from a picture.

It was years later when I finally understood the point Mom was making. Many draft dodgers did love their country and, along with the yellow race, they also deserved to be forgiven. All of us were hurt by the war, some killed, and some butchered like me. Others' lives were screwed up beyond repair.

Mom subdivided her heart into at least 10 parts, one for each of her nine children and of course, one for Dad. That day she only concentrated on the part reserved for me, and the conversation was focused on what I meant to her.

Mom lived for another 15 years after that conversation. We talked often about what was going on in our current lives, but never again talked about the war in such detail. Being a quiet woman, she listened more than she spoke, but she knew instinctively the right words to give her children.

It seems like mom's been gone forever. I miss her loving Irish heart, especially on Saint Patrick's Day. Mother was proud of three things: being Irish, being Catholic, and her children. She was a gentle, loving woman who asked God to watch over her children.

Her knowledge of matters of the heart were deeper than that of anyone else I've ever known. If I was working for the Veterans hospital trying to help young returning veterans, I'd hire mature Irish mothers to counsel them. I heard Rufus Wainwright express these words about his mother that touched my Irish heart: "You're born twice, once through birth, the second time when your mother dies."

My grandson, Tate, has inherited his great-grandmother's

Irish heart. At a very young age his emotional intelligence was obvious, and he knew without being taught what his role on this earth would be. As I watch him grow, it lifts my spirits to know that Mother's loving Irish heart will forever be with me.

Like his own mother, I know he will be involved in the love of mankind, using his time on earth to love, not hate others that share the planet with him.

My mother's conversation was fresh in my mind. I could now formulate a plan on how to get out of the hospital. I insisted that my doctors make some sort of decision, either cut off my other leg or change the plan of attack. Flushing the wound definitely wasn't helping.

The doctors all understood we had to go in another direction, even if it lead to an amputation. Finally, my doctors decided to close up the leg with a cast, then gave me powerful antibiotics. They changed the cast every two weeks or whenever it started showing green on the outside.

When they changed the cast, they'd clean up the area and recast the leg. My leg smelled so bad the guys would leave the room because they couldn't stand the stench. After several months, the bone healed and the antibiotics got ahead of the infection. The day finally came when they took off the cast for the last time.

I was happy because now I could start walking on my artificial leg. Of course it wasn't that simple, the foot had healed in a drop-foot position. My tendons had shortened in the back of my ankle, and they needed a couple of operations to lengthen them. Just a little more waiting while doctors worked their magic to get my ankle back to a walking position.

A brace was fitted quickly so we didn't lose any

range of motion. Walking started on parallel bars with a talented Physical Therapy Department. Every day my skills improved, and I progressed to crutches, a cane, and finally, walking solo. When I walked solo at first, I held out my arms to get my balance, just like a baby does when first walking.

The day finally came when I picked up my son and walked across the floor with him. Wow life's good! Shi was nervous, but knew I needed to continue to advance my walking skills. Our precious little boy was in no real danger. I would have broken any fall by landing on the artificial leg, saving him from injury.

We had won a big battle by saving one of my legs. Walking with two artificial legs is really tough. I was sort of walking okay, so it was time to venture out into the deeper water. Time to rent a small apartment just off base. To get out of the hospital for part of the day was therapeutic.

We were lonely, being so isolated from family and friends. We thought we could make new friends away from the hospital. There were other young couples from the hospital living in our complex. We would sit out on the lawn at night and talk with other young people.

We met this really neat gal who lived down stairs from us. She said her husband was coming home that weekend and it would be good for me to meet him.

About four o'clock on Friday afternoon, the meat wagon pulled up, so I got up to find out what was going on.

No problem, they were bringing her husband in on a gurney. The guy was paralyzed from the chest down. Was I thankful or what?

Another day, as my wife was wheeling me down the

hospital hallway in my wheelchair, we heard this guy say, "Could you help me?"

Shi stopped pushing me and went into the room. There was a young guy sitting in a wheelchair. He had both legs amputated above the knees, and it seemed as though he was also blind.

He asked her if she would please get a white shirt from his closet.

She did, he thanked her, and then he started to flirt with her a little.

She politely rebuffed his comments and we were on our way. I never spoke, and the poor guy didn't know he was flirting with a woman whose husband was no more than ten feet away. Was I thankful or what?

So you're not alone, and it could be worse! People are always telling that to people with disabilities, hoping that it might comfort them. I try to remember those guys on the bad days, hoping it will help. But realistically, suffering sucks.

Dealing with a major disability in life will never get easy, so be careful not to let the disability rule. You do not want to start a poison fruit tree orchard, then eat from it every day. Heck, look what happened to Adam and Eve from just one apple. Sometimes I wonder, what if I hadn't been wounded, and the killing would have continued for me. Would I have had a complete melt down? Gone mad like men that have committed horrible war crimes? That's the old, "what if" game I played. I hoped the humanity Mother taught me would have kicked in, rescuing me from the jaws of the monster this country was on their way to creating.

My tour in Vietnam was short, but it had an

unbelievable impact on my life. I'm thankful my tour of duty didn't have the chance to do more emotional harm. My acts were nothing compared to what the North Vietnamese Army did after we pulled out of the war.

They went on a rampage of killing that lasted for years. I understand their hatred for United States, but these killings were unnecessary. They piled up bodies until they had finally satisfied the right number of kills, which was known only to them.

Was it group madness fueled by revenge or a total breakdown of their morality? I wonder if they've ever heard that the sword of revenge has a curve in it, that while you're disemboweling your enemies, the sword is doing damage to you. I'm not sure how many were killed, but I understand fifty thousand Christians were slaughtered.

I believe so many years of foreign occupation had turned the North Vietnamese into ruthless savage killers. They couldn't stop themselves from killing. They played the blood sport for years until their rage finally cooled.

We also committed terrible acts of violence, like the Mỹ Lai Massacre, during the war. The level of humanity in war has huge swings, from giving out candy to children to burning them to death with bombs. These horrific acts are forgotten in less than a generation of life on the planet. So moms will be sitting at their son's beds crying a thousand years from now.

It's not our differences that fuel war, it's our likenesses. I don't believe the human race has evolved to a high enough level not to fight wars. We pray that countries who already have nuclear bombs will realize that war would be the end to all of us. Who really knows if they'd pull the trigger if push came to shove? I believe mankind is set on a course of self-destruction, unless he can learn to share the earth's resources.

In one of the episodes The Vietnam War, a documentary film by Ken Burns, it was stated that in the year of 1968 the 9th Infantry division killed almost 11,000 Vietnamese. And 50% of the kills were innocent civilians.

I'd alter his statement to say "innocent civilians *by day*." Of course the water buffalo could have been up all night setting those booby traps that blew off my leg. You did a great job, Ken, but I was there. A few hundred of the 9th Infantry division soldiers were also killed during that time. That's a forty five to one radio.

Of course the military counts were always padded, but it was still some ugly shit. For some inexplicable reason the North Vietnamese leaders decided to launch several offensives into the south. They were going to enlist local villagers and occupy certain strong holds. They may have gotten their inspiration from Washington, which sounds like something they'd do.

Big mistake. Our army, with the help of the South Vietnamese Army, was finally able to fight the war on our terms. We slaughtered them. Our troops became like a great swarm of killer bees traveling the country, stinging to death anything that moved. Honey bees would have known when to stop stinging.

When the North Vietnamese escalated the war, our troops turned up the violence like a bee hive of hybrid killer bees being disturbed. They defended the hive to a point way beyond what made sense.

Both sides were struggling to establish leadership, using fear as the vehicle to get the job done. The only way the North Vietnamese Army was going to take over the south was if we gave it to them. They had become over confident or didn't realize what damage the United States military was capable of. It's one thing to pick and choose your battles, it's another to go toe to toe with a military that will crush you.

They had a lot of little zipperheads (another dehumanizing term) brainwashed, ready to give their life for the cause. Our attitude was that we'd kill every last one of them if that's what it took.

Then one evening while the killer bees slept, our beautiful savior sprinkled a blanket of compassion over them. The next morning, when the sun came up over the rice paddies, there was no gunfire. Sounds of roosters crowing, birds singing, and children's voices as they tended their water buffalo was all that could be heard.

The guns were finally silenced. The great swarm of killer bees once again became honey bees. They began the work of developing the honey comb of a new nation. The horrible war had ended for us. We now could start the conversation with our mothers of how to heal our wounds.

7

PRESIDENT HERBERT HOOVER

*"Older men declare war. But it is the
youth that must fight and die."*

F INALLY, THE DAY CAME FOR MY RELEASE FROM
Fitzsimons Army Hospital in Denver, Colorado. That
sounded like I was getting out of prison.

The truth is, the staff was very dedicated, making it
hard to say good bye. Young highly intelligent folks were
in charge of getting me back on my feet. There was always
something going on, and the whole city of Denver seemed
to be supportive of the troops.

Playboy Bunnies would come out to the hospital just
to say hi and listen to the guys BS about their injuries.
Red Cross volunteers would take us down town to the
performing arts center, trying to educate us on the finer
things in life. Coors Beer Company provided us with free
beer, right at the hospital. Denver should be proud of the
way they treated the returning vets.

My hospital stay in Denver was from February to
October. Those were long difficult months, but finally it
was time to turn the page, to make the trip back home
to Wisconsin.

We loaded up all our worldly belongings in our rusty1964 Buick Special. I configured a makeshift bed for my little guy to sleep on, put that old Buick in drive and headed east. We were all excited.

I drove straight from Denver, Colorado to Racine, Wisconsin without stopping to sleep. We no longer had to put our lives on hold, waiting for some special date before going to the next step. We talked endlessly about our plans to establish roots. What was I going to do for a job? Where would we live? What a great feeling, just to be a family. We could now start, as they say, living the dream.

When we did get home our families gave us the support we needed to get settled in. It was a completely different story when it came to the community. The folks in Denver had spoiled me. I was under a false impression that everybody cared about us.

I remember thinking that the people in Wisconsin are a lot less supportive than the environment I had just come from. The country was in an uproar, coming apart at the seams. Young people were protesting the Vietnam War, demanding that we get out now. They were rightfully sick of the older generation's inability to end the war, refusing to accept the government's propaganda. The young people's mindset was, either the government was going to listen to their demands, or they would dismantle the whole system.

The young kids didn't take ownership of the war, they felt alienated from our process of governing. The protesting was their way of letting the government know they no longer would put up with endless demands on their generation to fight the Vietnam War. Many dropped out of the culture to develop their own subculture.

It was time for the government to start listening to the citizens who believed the war was wrong and had gone on much too long.

The government was starting to lose control of the citizens. They couldn't understand why Johnny didn't want to march off to war anymore.

Most of the older generation thought all young men should be sacrificed on the altar of war, except their sons. They believed that victory, or at least saving face at any cost, was our goal.

When Fred and Wilma Flintstone heard Pebbles chanting, "1, 2, 3, 4, we don't want you're fucking war," it made them think maybe the government was wrong. Of course, plenty of the older generation understood that it was impossible to fight another country's civil war, that the cost was greater than the prize.

I felt embraced by some and blamed by others, some young people believed I represented the government, which they hated. The older people were disappointed we hadn't delivered a victory for them.

I knew both young and old blamed me for the poor outcome of the war. It's like blaming a wife for being in the way of her drunken husband's fist when he beat's her up. If she would just learn to duck when he swung his fist she wouldn't have those black eyes, so really, it's her fault. People do not understand that the relationship is so unhealthily that she lacks the ability to end it.

When they blame me, I tried to stay out of the blowhard's conversation. You know, when people are talking their ignorant bullshit without any actual knowledge, it's best just to let them vent.

I wondered if they really thought about what impact

their comments had on a returning Vietnam veteran. When they saw me, it triggered a conversation either pro or con about the war.

People were angry and confused. They imagined sharing all that built-up frustration with me was the right thing to do. They thought I understood this country's misguided failed foreign policy better than they did. I became their conduit to send a message. I never figured out whether I should get the president on the phone or wait until my next meeting with him.

Well, they were wrong, and the last thing I wanted to talk about was that crazy war. My family had just gone through hell. We needed people to embrace us, not fight another war with them.

There were plenty of people who did embrace us, but I had to be careful to do a little fishing before I put my pole in the water with people. You never knew where the conversation would go, so it was smart to always be on guard. Keeping the war out of my life was all but impossible.

I did isolate myself from some people, but I'm not a big fan of isolation. It was better to deal with most of the assholes. To this day I will go out of my way to not let someone I'm unsure of know I served in the Vietnam War. I'm just not comfortable dealing with some of the remarks insensitive people can come up with. When asked to stand for recognition for serving my country, I do not stand. It draws sniper fire.

I understand that when the tea pot is left by itself on the stove, the pressure reaches the boiling point. School shootings are a good example of what happens to young men when they're isolated. Children who have some physical or emotional differences are isolated by classmates.

Most young men have never heard of the chicken effect. If there is a building full of young chickens and one has a little sore on its back the rest of the flock will pick at that sore until they kill the bird.

Teachers and parents are torn between allowing life to take its course and interfering. I'm unqualified to judge either of them. I can only imagine how difficult it can be to manage. Just like the chicken being picked to death, disabled vets are isolated by our society. What they need is the flock to stop picking at their sores, to be included in our culture.

When I came back to my family, I was still in the Vietnam "kill the Cong" mode. If the wind blew at night or I heard any loud noise, it would set me off. I would be up all night keeping watch for danger. Even my son's crying would set me off. I'd get nervous being around him.

I knew something wasn't right, but I figured things would improve over time. This kind of trauma needs time to heal and, as time passed, things did improve. I did my best to cope with life as it was, not as I wished it was. The scars were still there, but the skin had thickened to protect the injuries.

I needed to adjust to my new life, letting some of the brutality of the war slowly seep from my pours. Dealing with all the armchair quarterbacks giving me their low down on how we could have won the war was easy compared to dealing with memories of the war.

The people of Wisconsin seemed much less willing to help the returning veterans. We were someone to be suspicious of. Of course, there were people who cared deeply about us. I don't mean to diminish their help. My thoughts are more of a general feeling I was having at the time.

And who knows, maybe I was not reading the whole thing correctly. Emotions are difficult to assess when you're in the thick of things. It's a lot easier to assess in hindsight. Some help came in the form of advice, and other help came by what they didn't say.

You can talk the talk but many people never walked the walk. They never followed through with any real action.

I had this thing about not codling myself. I felt that could do more permanent damage. Poor me comes with a wheelchair. My father had raised a man, not a wimpy crybaby to be pitied.

I remember watching a movie on General Patton. He had belittled some soldier who was suffering from shell shock. That's what they called PTSD back in the Second World War. He was tougher than hell on them. It probably wasn't his greatest moment. Still, he expected his men to man up and they did. Nowadays, this kind of treatment is no longer acceptable from ranking commissioned officers.

I believe you need to accept help if you need it, but own your portion of fixing it. It's a cycle you see in welfare families. Once-proud people receive assistance from well-intentioned people, and four generations later, the family still requires assistance to survive. The Veterans Administration walks a very fine line as to how much help they should provide.

If they use too large of a paint brush when helping vets, it retards their development. A smaller brush with a few of the right hairs in it would be better. Of course the question is, how does a system that big tailor a cost-effective method of care to meet individual needs?

Cost-effective method is an oxymoron, never to be repeated when talking about the Veterans

Administration. Large organizations also tend to morph into practices that are more self-serving than a service to the veterans. Their original charter may have been to serve the wounded warriors, but they have been taken over by special interest groups. Once such groups have established a foothold in the organization, it's almost impossible to get rid of them.

In a computer you could reformat the hard drive, then reload the operating system. With the VA, that's not possible. Their mission is always changing, depending on what war or peace cycle the country is in. Our elected officials who really love their country, but want to get re-elected, make decisions based on what's good for their campaigns.

Why can't veterans join health care exchanges and go to the private sector for care? Most of the care the VA hospital provides to veterans is not service connected. The truth is, our society dumps the uninsured poor on the VA system. This overwhelms the VA as they do not have the correct resources to care for the wounded warriors. How an organization could get so screwed up is beyond my understanding.

Now, where was I before I got side tracked straightening out the VA hospitals?

Oh, I was looking for help.

I searched for help in churches, but they were busy taking care of the folks who looked like them and filled the plate on Sunday.

I took a look at the various veterans organizations, but it seemed to me they were mostly helping each other become drunks.

I finally returned to the gentle stream of my youth,

enlisting my family to give me the help I needed. Every one of my brothers and sister were there for me.

My sister Caroline and her husband Jim took us under their wing. Jim and I hit it off, and we spent many outings together discussing what had happened to me. If Jim watched a movie or a TV programs on Vietnam, he'd ask me to comment on it. This gave him the knowledge to understand what I'd had to deal with.

Most people imagine crazy guys sitting around in Vietnam drinking beer and smoking pot all day. Nothing could be further from what I experienced.

Our outfit had two pop coolers and one beer cooler. We had to put a guard on the two pop coolers. No one wanted the beer. The truth was, we were just half nuts, and drinking a pop after three days in the hot delta was all the excitement we needed. As far as smoking pot, I personally saw very little of it. The guys were so tired after long hot days and sleepless nights, they mostly needed rest.

You need to remember that whatever you're watching on the tube or big screen or reading in a book represents only the author's version of events. It's like a painting of the Grand Canyon. If you really want to see the place, it's best to take a trip. My advice is if you're not a veteran and haven't walked in their shoes, it's not okay to voice your opinion. Remember, not every idea that comes into your head needs to be expressed.

This country had handed all its problems of the war over to young people like me. Then, when we came back they handed the complex problems of caring for the vets to the VA. They didn't understand that neither the VA nor the veteran should be asked to do it alone.

Uncle Sam needs to partner with the citizens if there is

going to be any chance to successfully deal with post war problems. Believe it or not, you need to help us with the security of this great nation.

These men and women are fighting wars for you. Your name is on the bullets that do the killing. Maybe you believe wars are like after a big football game. Now that it's over, we'll all shake hands and become friends, because after all, it's only a game.

Next season we will be at war with the brown people. We will make up names to call them, like Rag Head, Camel Driver, or Terrorist. When it's over, you'll shake hands and wait for another president to suck us into another war.

But it's not over for many; they'll have to deal with the war injuries for the rest of their lives.

When I came home, I had personalized the war. If you're a veteran reading this, remember, do not allow the blood of this nation's enemies to stain the fabric of your soul. The blood is too concentrated for you to deal with. Allow the nation to dilute the blood. It's on the country's hands, not yours. You only carried out their wishes.

Things get messy, and sorting out the ones who deserve killing or who don't is hard under the best conditions. I'm pretty sure that I would never have taken another person's life if it wasn't forced on me by this country.

There are rules of engagement that soldiers must follow. I did my best to honor those rules. Even if I had broken them, the blood was still on this country's hands. Whatever the soldiers did in Vietnam doesn't compare to the sins of the politicians who used the war for their political gain. I hope all of them are in hell.

Ah, but so many lambs must be scarified on the altar of war in every generation. The war dogs need to be satisfied.

By the time I got home, the government's support for the Vietnam War was getting shakier by the day, even with the money folks. The changes in the draft laws were starting to affect the rich folks. They now had a dog in the fight. All of a sudden, they decided the war was only worth poor kid's lives, not the elitists.

They started thinking deep thoughts like, does the war strengthen our nation's security? Could the money being spent on the war be used for a better purpose? What are we accomplishing and where does it all end? Is this country totally broken? If things do not change, will the country collapse?

The seeds were finally planted for the eventual pullout of the troops from the Vietnam War.

Our role in the Vietnam War was difficult to understand. Before our involvement they had to drive the French out. That caused a leadership vacuum that ended up in a civil war. Then we got involved causing the civil war to continue and be combined with a war of independence from foreign occupation.

To this day, our government has some misguided illusion that they can dismantle another country's government and install our form of governing. To this I say, they're nuts. It would be much better to leave whatever government is in place, then work to move the leadership in a positive direction.

For years we had poured money into training the South Vietnamese Army, which in the end produced nothing but a lot of dead American boys. Why do you think this is true? I believe it's because our country takes too small of a view of the complex power struggle that exist in the world. Their civil war had just been delayed for 10 years. Nothing had changed. The question of who was going to run the country still needed to be sorted out. Every 19 year old kid in my outfit knew the South Vietnamese Army was rotten from the top down.

On the other hand, the North Vietnamese Army wanted victory at any cost. They had the leadership to motivate their soldiers to get the job done. America provided the North Vietnamese Army with the motivation they needed to win the war. They had their hatred of us to rally their forces into action.

That's very similar to our own nation's birth. We had the British to hate, giving us one common cause to accomplish. Vietnam is a very poor, over-populated country. The seeds of war were planted in the ground of poverty. The fight for who was going to control what little harvest those seeds produced was their civil war.

One of the best things that came from the war was that the nation was unified under one central government. That's an important factor if a nation is to put down its weapons and establish some common purpose.

I don't believe the Communist form of government is great, but it's a lot better than being a colony of another country. Distribution of the country's power is at least an internal problem. Their answer to this problem is ruling with an iron fist. Of course, if they ever want to fully develop their people, they'll have to loosen the strangle hold, allowing oxygen to flow to the citizens' brains.

Look at the example of North Korea's concentration of power and South Korea's open society. Being so isolated, it's not surprising that a dictator would become unbalanced. We surround Kim Jong-un with our military, and he responds with force. We try to control other nations with our Defense Department, which can only be done by threatening weaker nations. If we ever want to get out of places like South Korea we'll need the services of the State Department.

For many years the U.S.A. and China have interfered in the creation of one Korea. Seems to me, the first countries that should talk are the U.S.A. and China. We need to encourage the two halves to become a whole, finding a path to a united Korea. First a baby creeps, then it crawls, next it walks, and finally it becomes a long distance runner. This requires a generational view of development of human rights.

By using our military we get to enjoy all those veterans' memorial walls with the names of our beloved sons and daughters, brothers and sisters, husbands and wives, fathers and mothers and friends on them. For almost half of my life we have been at war. Is there no end to this wall building?

I remember caring people like Jane Fonda, trying to change the conversation of war. For this, she was villainized. I always thought of her as a person who loved her country deeply. Her commitment to end the war was commendable. Of course she was young and innocent and didn't realize you cannot change a mindset until the student is ready.

For me, forgiving my country for their ignorance is something I work on daily. There never was that moment when the heavens cleared, rays of light beamed down on me, and I was born again. In my early years, I believed the Vietnam War topped the list of the dumbest things this country has ever done. I now understand after what's happened in the Middle East that it's just part of a long history of flawed thinking in our country.

Life's events still can affect how I deal with my emotions. If I'm having an especially tough time with my leg, it has an impact on me. I'm best at keeping the demons under control when body, mind, and spirit are in balance. The more I discipline myself, the easier life becomes. The problems are always with me, so the best I can do is be as healthy and as strong as possible to deal with them. Having a disability gives one an opportunity for real growth. The trouble is, some day's I'd much rather let the armchair quarterback grow and take a vacation from all this suffering.

A minister once told me, if I just lay it at the foot of the cross, I can live with anything. The saying goes, "God doesn't give you any more to deal with than you can handle." Really? This is the challenge that every human on the planet deals with. How do we keep from being taken over by things that seem beyond our circle of understanding?

Understanding—that is the key word. We need to practice living life in a manner that will open us to the knowledge that will sustain us during our journey through life. You have to become acquainted with your demons. Invite them to come out of the dark places in your mind.

Your demons are like parasites, enjoying life at the expense of the host. Once they're identified, you can develop a plan to deal with them.

What was the scariest thing you can remember as a child? Was it the monster under the bed or the creature in the closet? Once Mother shone a flashlight on them, these imaginary monsters disappeared. The next night the same thing would happen, and when did they disappear? Your mother got you over this fear of the dark by gently, patiently, reasoning with you until your mind could absorb her knowledge.

Maybe you need to talk with someone who has slept under the bed or in the closet, who knows how to deal with demons. Unlike these imaginary monsters, your disability will provide you with real monsters to deal with. They come from coping with extreme physical and emotional living conditions. You must learn to hold your demons close, get a head-lock on them. Don't mask their existence with booze, drugs, or self-destructive behavior.

Those solutions don't work, but are used by the general populations who are healthy. They act like a child applying a bandage to their forehead to cure a headache.

If demons are exposed, you can use them to deal with life's challenges. I find by quieting my mind and focusing on what is tormenting me I'm able to understand the demon's place in my life. My demons will always be waiting under the bed or in the closet.

The trick is to get them to hold the flashlight for me.

8

PRESIDENT JOHN ADAMS

"Great is guilt of an unnecessary war."

I HOPE ALL THOSE LITTLE CHURCHY FOLKS WHO sat on the draft board are satisfied. They almost got me killed fulfilling my military obligation. I now had earned the right to be called a baby killer. The term "draft dodger" would never be uttered in my direction again.

I really needed to get to know my son Shawn, who was just a few months old when I got home. Shi and I were married only three days before my forced slavery into the army. We were both lonely, tired of handling what life was giving us by ourselves. All three of us needed face time to become a family.

I was feeling cheated for not being home at my son's birth. The war had pulled on our family until we both felt like we were coming apart at the seams. I was afraid to show any weakness but was a total wreck physically and mentally.

I figured that I could pick up all the broken pieces, rejoining the world I left two years earlier. I was under a false impression that not much had changed. I was nervous about how people would accept my disability, and I was also concerned about how I would support my family.

Family and friends all had ideas on how I should put my life back together. Some felt going to school was the right thing, but before my injuries I hadn't considered that option. I didn't know which course of study I should pursue. Would they want me to become a rocket engineer or maybe a scientist?

Well, I would have to ponder my options. If I'd had those options earlier, I wouldn't have been enslaved in the military service in the first place.

Of course, they didn't realize that it's easy to tell someone else what to do with their lives. Most of them had no idea what to do with theirs.

It would take some time to process such a life changing event, time to get my head pointed in a different direction. I'd spend twenty years of my life on a small creek leading to the sea, only to find out that now I had to start my journey over. On the outside I tried to put on a good show, but inside it was, *What should I do with my life?*

After a couple of months of listening to all the advice, I decided to visit my old employer. I worked in a factory prior to being drafted with only a poor high school education. The job market was lousy for poor folks. I would have taken any job they offered.

The Human Resources Manager and another company lackey were interviewing me and being very careful not to say the wrong thing. They danced around the subject of my disability like a new car sales manager working the buyer with his flunky sales person.

They kept looking back and forth at each other trying to figure out if there was a way the company could get out of giving me my job back. After a half-hour, these two clowns couldn't find a way out, so they gave up and finally offered me my old job back. I agreed.

The very next day I was there bright and early, ready to work on the paint line. After eight hours of painting garbage disposals, I was totally wiped out.

When I got home I tried to get up the stairs of the apartment we were renting, but I couldn't raise my leg far enough to make a step. After 15 minutes of trying, I sat down and pulled myself up the stairs backwards.

Shi took one look at me and said there was no way I could do that job. And it dawned on me—I had missed the point. My mind was ready for work, but my body had different ideas.

We talked about the job situation that night. We came up with the idea that if I explained things, the company would help.

Early the next day I went to see the Human Resources Manager. My original vibes were telling me something was wrong, but still I pleaded my case. I asked if there was some other kind of job I could do for them?

"No," he said, "not at this time."

I thought, Right, maybe when I grow my leg back!

This guy of course, was just the messenger. The company set the policies, and he implemented them. I was just a young guy, but the message came through loud and clear. They were dumping me because of my disability. My status had changed. I no longer was part of the company's team. I was an outcast, treated the way lepers were treated in biblical times.

I didn't understand how they could be so heartless, but I knew one thing for sure: I wouldn't beg these pigs for a job. I had been weakened by the war and didn't have the maturity or strength to fight them. I'm sure they were thinking what good little boys they were to have gotten rid of the company's obligation. After all, they weren't a charity. If this guy wants a different job, he'd better be the best qualified.

I thought that many of the best-qualified dodged the draft and spent their time in colleges while the blue collar scum like me got our asses blown off in Vietnam. So you and that other best-qualified boy go to church this Sunday and tell each other what good boys you are. Better yet, just skip church; go golfing with some of the best-qualified people in that little circle you imagine is life.

It was an important lesson to learn. My ridiculous idea that InSinkerator Manufacturing was going to help me had been corrected, their position clarified. It was never about those pigs helping me reestablish myself in the community. It was about the big hogs crowding out the disabled veterans, leaving no room at the trough to feed.

I could not believe I'd been so stupid to expect them to take any responsibility for the war. Those self-centered bastards sat around college campuses pissing away the taxpayer's money, while the poor of the nation died in the swamps of Vietnam. It's kind of like the line from Charlie Daniels song "Long Hair Country Boy": "A rich man goes to college and a poor man goes to work."

The North Vietnamese Army treated me better than those sons of bitches.

"Wow," my wife Shi would have said, "could you get another swear word in your venting?"

I've always wanted to give the middle finger to those boys at InSinkerator Manufacturing, so consider it done.

And I never owned a garbage disposal. I'd rather eat the garbage than give them any money. Did all young well connected men in our country think this way? Of course not, I can only speak to my experiences.

My mind was once again consumed with how I was going to get my life back into some sort of order. We hadn't received any disabled veteran's pension and were in serious need of some cash.

The next month Shi was fortunate enough to land a job, so we didn't have to go on welfare. That would have been a blow to my family's recovery. I believe it was six months before we received our first veteran's pension check.

I always wondered why the United States Army would discharge a severely disabled veteran without any way of supporting himself. You would think they could continue your military pay until the VA got their act together. This was the first example of many more to come of the VA's inability to meet the vet's needs.

I'm so stupid. For years I actually expected that someone at the VA could help me with the problems that came with being disabled. We survived with the help of family and friends. It was easy for the company to treat me poorly and for the well-connected rich to avoid my fate by pulling strings to get themselves out of the military.

Now, avoiding life's disasters completely is another story. Someday they too could suffer some disaster that is out of their control. Maybe they'll get sick, have a child born with some impairment. Could be their only sin is that they're getting a little older and the company decides to dump them for a cheaper model. They'll find themselves on the outside, wondering why life has been so unfair to them.

I think of what is said about veterans who have served

their country: "All gave some, some gave all." With the well-connected rich, it should be, "They did all they could to fill their pockets at the expense of the weak and poor of the world."

These days companies are much worse. They've destroyed many more people in their relentless quest to fill the pockets of the well-connected elitists. It's gotten to the point where the nation's solvency is at risk of collapsing from corporate greed. By outsourcing jobs to the lowest bidders they will destroy our country. Take one look at Detroit and tell me this isn't true!

Companies are ignorant, not understanding their role in making this country work. They have a misguided attitude that they don't need to be good citizens.

I liken these companies to a pack of wolves, circling the earth looking for the poor. When they find a place where human beings can be exploited, they set up shop, killing off the jobs somewhere else. At first their actions affected a small minority of people that couldn't keep up with the herd. As time went on, the wolf packs kept getting bigger, and now large numbers of people are feeling the pain.

The outcome will be certain: the culture will be destroyed. Folks will have no choice but to live a poorer lifestyle. Politicians have been brainwashed into believing operating on a world market makes the nation stronger.

Foreign trade's street name is invasive species. There is an order in nature that has evolved to keep things in balance, but it hasn't evolved equally over the whole planet. If they are going to build $100 tennis shoes in Vietnam, they need to also sell them there. Trading with other nations is a very complex endeavor, which can't be left in the hands of companies.

The same is true in the relationship between jobs and the survival of our citizens. It's just a matter of time before the country is sucked lifeless by invasive species. In this country, 90% of the wealth is in the hands of 10% of the people. My guess is that most of the returning veterans are not in that 10% class.

The lesson here is that companies abuse their power. They are happiest when they can maintain a permanent underclass of workers. They truly are classless pigs, only seeing life through a prism of the dollar. We need to rebuild the middle class if there is to be a healthy nation. The plantation mentality is how this country started out; will it be how it ends?

There has to be some reasonable balance of wealth distribution in this country. I understand, not all folks are equally gifted. Still, isn't there a way to share the wealth? We need to find ways of reconnecting the front office with the factory floor. All employees need to have some skin in the game. This would put the responsibilities and rewards where they belong, on the employees.

The flow of our nation's wealth needs to find the natural course to the citizens' hands. It's now paid in as taxes, and then filtered back through government programs to the workers. Maybe this is a description of socialism, or one of those isms.

If rich folks only represent 10% of the population, how do they get elected to office? Republicans get elected by focusing mostly on three made up concerns: God, guns and gays.

They also often have a couple of off-the-wall feel-good concerns of the times. It could be some stupid idea about lowering taxes or closing loop holes. We all know the only way to lower taxes is for all citizens is to cut expenses. It's not shifting taxes from the rich to the middle class or borrowing money for our grandchildren to pay current expenses. It would help if Jesus would come back and chase the lobbyist from Washington.

By concentrating on the 3G's they picked up the vote from good folks confused by what the real concerns are in their lives. They've always painted themselves as the conservative party and lately have split into two parties, one being extremely ultra-conservative. You know, the ones with the real values that the rest of the citizens can't understand. They believe they are chosen from God as the enlightened ones. Just listen to them. After all, they have a moral obligation to judge the rest of the world.

I say if the founding fathers wanted all you Godly assholes running Washington, they wouldn't have written into the constitution to separate religion from state.

At the end of President Bush's term, I believe we were only a few months from a depression that would have made the 1929 crash look like a speed bump. So how could the party with all the best qualified CEOs in it, bankrupt the country? Was it Bush's fault alone? No, it was something he inherited from President Reagan.

Remember, Reagan started the movement to deregulate the banks and Wall Street, and screwed employees out of their pension by starting 401k plans. They could finally steal with one hand tied behind their back. Following his presidency, weakening of regulations continued until the bankers, brokers and employers were allowed to steal with both hands.

It took years for the hopes and dreams of President Reagan to be realized. Along the way, the dream turned into a nightmare. Banks needed bailouts from taxpayers, and unregulated Wall Street brokers led to a meltdown in the financial markets. Grandparents ended up living below the poverty line because of unfunded retirement plans. Thirty-some years later, we are still dealing with the fallout from his wrongheaded thinking.

The country is starting to look like an old shirt that's been jerked between two puppies, one named republican and the other named democrat. They are both dogs, pandering to whoever will feed them. Democrats and republicans have to refine their skills to become world class thinkers, coming up with new ways of governing the complex world we live in.

Certainly, our representatives need to think outside of a four year term and their party's affiliation. Because the legislation they pass today will affect our grandchildren. They won't be democrats or republicans; they'll be babies. It's like hurting one's back, you feel okay today but can't get out of bed tomorrow morning. Shallow thinkers pass bills that feel good today, but years later really hurt our nation.

Another caution to the rich—you will only steal so much from the poor before they will rise up and put an end to you. The poor will over throw our government if they are not allowed to share in its wealth. The unrest that grew more violent each year during the Kennedy, Johnson, and Nixon presidencies will reappear. It's my opinion that either the wealth comes back to the people or the system will collapse.

The younger vets might get a little more respect because 9/11 brought things into focus for a lot of Americans. Not to worry though, the politicians have short memories and are in the pockets of the companies. Veterans will seamlessly go from being heroes to being burdens on the taxpayers.

In a couple of years when the war ends, they'll be looking at ways to cut taxes and your name will come up. They won't call you a war hero or a veteran. You'll become part of the entitlement scum of the earth. When the rich no longer want to face the truth, they will come up with excuses why they shouldn't be asked to pay the bills for the poor.

I'm painting the companies with a very large black paint brush. Certainly there are companies who deserve better. I realize that if you gave ten kids a quarter a piece, by the end of the day one or two of them would have all the quarters. That's why young professionals should be taught to take only what they need. They have a bigger role on this earth than to fill their pockets at the expense of the poor.

So how does one survive in such a nasty environment?

The truth is, most people don't, and families are failing because all the bread is in the king's company's hands. There is nothing left but moldy bread crumbs for the peasants. I believe it takes years for companies to ruin our way of life, but they will do it in your life time.

Now that I've explained to you how our system operates, I'll tell you how I overcame it. I was forced into rethinking my options, which were either getting some additional education or start gaming our system.

In the fall of that year, I started school to make myself marketable for a job. It did work for me. I was able to land a job in a fairly good company. Education did work, but I wished I'd taken more time to explore my options. I believe what I really needed to do is identify my strengths, putting the disability on the back burner.

The question that needed to be answered was, What did I want to do with my life before I became disabled? Could I achieve my life's dreams while being disabled? Will education work for the returning veteran nowadays? It might, but it's a dog-eat-dog culture we live in. The only way to the top is over the bodies of the weak. You'll have to define what doing well means, and get real.

Let me explain what getting real means. Say you're not college material. Admit it, don't waste your time beating your head against the wall. I see so many young kids going to college because Uncle Sam is paying the bill. Colleges can charge any price and produce nothing because they're not held accountable by the students or taxpayers. They oversell their degree programs. After 4 years, grads are wondering why they can't get a job in underwater basket weaving. Before entering any course of study, one needs to ask if it comes with French fries.

Young people have some false impression that throwing someone else's money at their life decisions will clarify their journey.

Well, you have to learn about money before anything else. Who's the thief? How do they steal money from the poor of this nation? It's not a guy in a dark alley with a gun that threatens you. It's the gal in the blue suit lending you money.

Most human beings have no idea who they are, so they look to the culture to help define their life story. The banks partner with colleges, car companies, real estate brokers and any other outfit selling over-hyped merchandise. The people selling the hype are the real crooks, but banks are driving the getaway car. If you shake hands with a banker, when you're done, you'd better check to see if you have all your fingers.

The education system in America tells our youth they can be anything they want to be. Does that make sense? Did you ever see a pack of toy poodles pulling a dog sled? You'd be better off getting real and making sure your money is being spent correctly. Take time to develop obtainable goals. There's no hurry, because colleges will take your money at any age. There are colleges, technical schools, and many businesses to help you obtain your goals, but get real.

When you land a job, show up early, leave late, no fake migraines. Work your butt off and show them you're really a grounded good employee. I'm saying, take those stupid piercings out of your face, dress appropriately, don't sleep with the boss, and conduct your affairs like a grown up. You're a full grown person, not a kid anymore, so either conform to the work place or starve.

This is your opportunity to lay down a good work record. Don't you think someone will notice and help you with your journey? "Please" and "Thank you" are always nice touches. Didn't the service teach you about showing respect for rank? Four things determine how you're going to advance in the work place. They are attitude, attitude, attitude and ability.

When I came back from the war, the VA tested me and decided I'd make a good accountant or a computer programmer. Well, that was a crock, but they didn't know me. So why would I be looking at them to tell me who I was?

They were, of course, looking at the disability and not what I really was. If they'd known the right questions to ask, they would have found out that I had a really strong desire to work in the housing industry.

I was young and confused by all that had happened to me. I thought my disability had changed the person I had grown up to be. My disability had messed with my self-confidence, and I was unsure about my future.

This brings me to another example of the VA not understanding their role in helping the returning vets. They need to refine their system to better understand the veterans before giving out career advice. I'd suggest in their evaluation of returning veterans they interview family, teachers, clergy, friends, and other people who knew the person all of their life.

This is one of those moments in life that the V A should try to get it right if they're interested in really helping the vets. Young veterans coming home disabled really need to be dealing with the real deal, not some wannabe counselor. For every dollar they'd spend up front, they'd save thousands on the backside. They throw away money on educating veterans for jobs they'll never be successful at.

Thinking back on my children's journey to achieve their career goals helps me understand the process more clearly. I had a strong desire to see both of my children graduate from college. It was on the top of my bucket list. They started out like most young people, exploring their opportunities of how to fulfill their parent's dreams. It took many trials and errors, and the path was long and painful for all of us.

The problem was, I did not understand that they weren't ready for higher education yet. They needed time to mature and set some goals for themselves. Why did I think it was so important for them to finish college? It was because I did not want them to become cannon fodder for the government or companies like I had. They did graduate from college, but it was on their time frame, not mine.

Lots of young guys choose the military instead of starting a career, and for many that only kicks the can down the road. When they're done with the service, they still need to go through the process that my children went through. And if you have career-changing injuries, it further complicates the choices.

The military service can be a negative experience for many. The military replaces a young person's parents, telling them what to do for three or four years. I believe service to your country works best at no more than four years. After that there is twenty years of kicking the can down the road. Did you grow up or did you just prolong your childhood?

Time to get real. No more running in place. You must go forward even if it kills you. If you run into a wall then you have to figure out a way over, around or through it. No more baby steps for you. It's time for big boy steps that will take you out of your comfort zone.

My son taught me a good lesson about building a career. He started out working contract jobs, working only a few months on a special project for different companies. After five years of doing this he had a lot to offer anybody. Now companies seek him out and he is very marketable.

It's not like he was on an expressway traveling at 70 miles per hour toward his final destination. It's more like he was on a country road with lots of stops along the way. He needed to get out of the old pickup truck every so many miles and have a conversation with the local boys about where the fishing might be good.

Maybe if he took the old gravel road outside of town he'd find something that pleased him. The destination point should keep moving until you feel that things are right for you. Take your shoes off. Let the earth seep between your toes. Is this a place where you could send out starter roots? If you do, the roots will either grow healthy or they will die from being planted in the wrong soil.

Young people need to find their place on the planet. The answers come from not only your journey but also from the journeys of others.

Most of the problems come from too much structure in a young person's life. My children were in sort of a developmental prison for the first 18 years of their lives. They mostly followed my leadership to some predetermined goal setup by our educational system. Once they got away from my control they began to spread their roots and eventually became beautiful flowering plants.

Of course, hindsight is 20-20. What I wished I had done is let them begin their journey much younger. The trick of being a good parent is to let the child have just the right amount of freedom. Too much freedom can result in major problems, but not enough freedom will limit their growth.

We all grow together. So young parents are challenged to be experts at things they are still learning. I believe that's why young parents need to hang with grandparents or seniors. It is necessary to complete the circle of life. I still consult with a friend who is 85 years old. I find his knowledge very insightful. If you seek the truth, your mind will eventually pull the curtain to unveil who you are.

Be ready. Keep your fishing pole on a rack just behind the pickup seat. If you see an old timer fishing, stop and ask how the fishing in this stream is. Maybe he'll teach you how to catch whatever fish lives in that stream. Don't be overly judgmental about his fishing style, because new disciplines take time to make sense.

After you taste the fish from this stream, you'll either acquire a taste for them or it will be time to move on to try another stream. Eventually, you'll come upon a stream where the fish are to your liking and settle for a while. Some will fish many streams before they find where they belong. Others will settle after only a few attempts. Neither is wrong. It all depends on what gifts or challenges life has given them.

9

GENERAL GEORGE S. PATTON

"A pint of sweat saves a gallon of blood."

IT'S TIME FOR A FAMILY STORY. SO LEAN BACK on the fishing stool and I'll tell you about my cousin.

She was single most of her life, needing to take care of herself. She studied to be a beautician and began dolling up the gals around town.

Her father, who was a very shrewd business man, bought an older home on Main Street. He let her operate her business out of half of the main floor. The other half they turned into another space for a business.

Then they built two smaller apartments upstairs. Wow, three reasonably priced spaces for rent on Main Street. She made over a $1,000 a month on just the rent. So her first haircut starts at $1,015.00.

My niece also became a beautician. She started out by renting a store for $1,500 a month. She worked hard, long hours and did a good job for her customers.

One day I was visiting her, and she told me she couldn't make a go of it. I shared the story of our cousin with her, and she realized the two business models were $2,500 per month apart.

Doing the math, $2,500 divided by $15.00 per haircut equals 166 haircuts per month. And if you divide 166 by 23 working days per month, that's 7 haircuts a day before she became even with my cousin. After working for the first 3 to 4 hours a day, she arrived at $0.00.

It seems simple, but most young people starting their life forget to do the math.

My cousin wore many hats in her life, she was a landlord, a banker, a general contractor, or whatever else she needed to be to run a business. If her roof needed replacing, she'd go to the discount store to buy roofing, then hire some retired guy to put it on. It goes without saying, the roof would be paid for when it was put on.

She didn't believe in letting bankers use her to make them rich. If she needed a car, she'd investigate until she found the very best car for the money, then pay cash for it. Her favorite hat was her beautician's hat, but she realized she needed to keep the other hats in her closet to make a living. If you're shopping for education or pantyhose, you'd better have something under your hat besides a credit card.

Don't get all impressed by some bank giving you a loan for an over-valued product. Banks act as front men for the wealthy, and getting a loan means you get to carry the water for the rich folks. The least you can do to help yourself is borrow money for things that are going to make life better. That's reasonably priced education, houses, land or a business.

Do not borrow money to finance vacations, cars, big girl/boy toys or anything that's on its way to becoming worth zero. If you just can't help yourself from dealing with banks, buy some stock in a Canadian bank. They'll pay you a nice dividend and they're as safe as it gets.

I believe loans retard human development, so don't let a credit card company manage your financial affairs. You'll be their dog, living just outside the comfort of the camp fire. They'll eat steak and throw you the bone.

If you become too bold and want a whole steak for yourself, remember what is said about old mushroom hunters. There are old mushroom hunters, and there are bold mushroom hunters. But there are no old bold mushroom hunters around the rich folk's camp fire.

In this country, our citizens believe they do not have to understand finances. Just getting the right degree or job will make their life go right. Well, boys and girls, I'm telling you they're wrong, that we all need to minor in finances. No matter what you do for a living, you'll have to understand the role of money in your life.

Stand around a farmers' market almost any place in the world, you'll hear the locals negotiating the price of produces. That's because they live in the real world. They can make the association of the value to the labor. When they immigrate to the United States, in five years they manage to own two restaurants and a home in the suburbs.

On the other hand, many of our folks drive around in large expensive SUVs, doing their best to warm up the planet. Two weeks after they lose their jobs, they sign up for welfare benefits. The SUV is repossessed after a couple missed payments, three months later they've moved back in with their parents. They've financed everything. Even borrowing against any equity increases of the home the bank owns. Remember, there is a king's ransom to be paid for that castle.

My son was visiting from Minneapolis. He said, "Dad, where is the Starbucks in this town?"

I said, "There is none. For what it cost for coffee at Starbucks, the truck stop will give you two eggs, bacon, toast *and* coffee. The younger generation thinks they are living large. That's because the banks have developed a business model that strips them of their hard earned money. Really, they're brainwashed, living a poorer life in the long run.

Remember, a banker's only product is your money. They often produce misery, instead of wealth for their clients.

Panda bears that eat mostly bamboo credit cards are always on the endangered list, just hanging on by their teeth. Now really, how much fat can a Panda put on, eating bamboo?

The momma brown bear teaches her clubs to eat almost any rich cache of food they can get their paws on. They build up reserves of fat so when the winter winds blow, they can take a nap and live off their cash.

What is the longest time period a person who operates with cash can be broke? If they get paid weekly, it's until Friday. What is the longest time period a person who operates on credit can be broke? Doesn't matter how often they get paid, it's until they're dead or maybe a little after their death.

So by all means get that great job, but use the money you earn to serve your needs, not the needs of some lazy fat-ass banker.

10

SENATOR
ROBERT M. LA FOLLETTE

*"In times of peace, the war party insists on making
preparation for war. As soon as prepared
for it, insists on making war."*

LEADERSHIP WAS ONE OF THE MOST
important traits for me to consider when I was
trying to get my life on track. The people you associate
with during your formative years makes a difference.

We all want to think of ourselves as standalone self-
made individuals, but actually many good people go into
getting the recipe just right. It's like making a great batch
of cookies. All the steps have to be understood, the ingredients have to be weighed, the oven temperature adjusted,
and the timer set. The quality of ingredients needs to be
very good. If junk goes in the oven, junk comes out of
the oven.

A parent building a great leader is like putting together
a puzzle of a thousand pieces. When you first start, it's just
a pile of pieces. You begin by turning every piece right side
up. Wow, lots of pieces! What should I look for?

I'll look for the outside corners or edges that are straight. They should be easy to find. You now have the outside parameters identified and can began to fill in spaces using that information. You now cherry pick all the easily identifiable shapes or colors.

Next, the real hard work comes when you're in the blue water or sky. Everything looks alike. Looking closer, you see the water is a little darker blue than the sky. So, you divide those colors, but still there are a lot of pieces that look alike.

When children are born, the process is similar. They require loving, caring parents to assemble the pieces. At some point, the community joins in to support the family. This interaction with schools, churches, supportive family and friends helps build the children into leaders. If the children have a steady footing and continue to receive the needed encouragement, they have the chance to become leaders. Children also need to see good examples of leadership.

Remember that puzzle? What if, when you were putting it together there wasn't a picture on the box to look at? If you drop the puzzle on the floor while it's being put together, what happens? Some of the pieces break apart, and you carefully reassemble them. Our lives are full of job losses, failed marriages, sickness, and who knows what's coming next?

These events can influence the family's wellness, but they do not have to deliver a killing blow to your mission of building a leader. Just keep your eye on the prize, and don't let these hiccups affect the final goals.

The company that I landed my first job with had a chief engineer that I looked up to. My first dealing with

Jim was right after I became a draftsman. I worked 4 days a week and went to school on the fifth day. This went on for three long years, and finally I finished my studies.

I was making half the salary I was worth, so it was time to ask for a raise. I felt confident my immediate boss, who was not the chief engineer, knew my value to the engineering team and would see to it that I was paid a fair wage. I sat down and pleaded my worth for over an hour.

He gave me all the double talk bullshit about why it couldn't happen now. They were a cheap outfit that shared the money with their company lackeys.

I wasn't good at ass kissing. I felt disrespected, so I told him I'd be leaving in two weeks. I had worked hard for three years for very little pay, and I was doing better work than his senior draftsmen. The company was doing well because of hard working guys like me, not because of those lackeys that golf with each other.

He was a good enough guy, but he never really understood that timing is important when managing employees.

Well, in a couple of days his boss, Jim, our chief engineer, called me into his office. He asked what would it take to keep me with the company.

Before I could answer, Jim said, "How about $300.00 a month?"

I replied, "Yes." Because I really only wanted $150.00. I think he knew that, but when he did things, he didn't play games like my direct supervisor.

The company had finally shown me the respect I was due by paying me the salary of a draftsman. Jim understood that I was equal to my co-workers, not some kid in training. He understood how a man operates.

After that my wages were kept in line with my

responsibilities. Some years later I began to feel unimportant, not part of the team again. There were others who felt the same way. You know the feeling: What am I doing with my life?

Jim picked up on this. He started sending the young guys to the many production plants we had. This clarified our role, we became part of the Engineering Team. Most leaders allow things to fester, but not Jim. He came up with solutions to problems before they got out of hand.

Now we fast forward. I'd been there several years, and I really needed to be rewarded for my hard work.

Once again, Jim sensed it was time to promote me and he did just that. He had to be a very busy man with the job of chief engineer, but always kept his eye on all the personnel under him. He somehow knew when he was needed. He took the time to show the leadership required to run a company.

The guy just got it. He's someone you can take an order from because you respect him. He went to college to become an engineer, but he also served in the Army. Jim was an officer in the Second World War, commanding infantry soldiers. He never talked about his military service, but I knew he had been through hell for his country. He was the greatest leader that I have personally known in my life. He encouraged everyone around him to do their best. I knew I was in the company of a great man.

True to form, Jim spent his final days tending to his wife, who had become too frail to take care of herself. After his wife went to be with our lord, he spent a little time in a lovely veteran's home before joining her.

How did Jim get to be such a great leader? Well, he probably started out life as a really promising guy. There was the war and his country needed him, so he was commissioned by the army to be an officer. The army does a good job at giving officers the in-the-box leadership education, which means thinking outside of the box is frowned upon.

Certainly being a field commander of infantry troops in a war zone honed his leadership skills. When the war was over, he understood that to be a great leader, he needed to get away from the in-the-box leadership constraints of military life.

There have been many great leaders that have come from the military, but I'd guess they would have been even greater if they would have had the freedom required for real growth. Military service adds to a person's ability to be a good leader, teaching discipline, honor, responsibility and so on.

But there will come a day—and it's different for everyone—when these teachings fall short from what it really takes to become a great leader. In many cases the officer is ready for advancement with no place to put him, so he has all these dead periods during his career.

With no place to go, he burns up his time, running in place. Once in a while we will get into a war that will provide him with a platform to grow. Imagine a little pony put into a circus. There is a ring he must run around, performing different ticks before he gets his sugar cube. This ring is not very big, and soon the pony becomes bored to death waiting to perform in the big top.

Now if the pony was a mustang running free over thousands of acres, he wouldn't know those stupid tricks, but he'd know much more about survival.

For another example of leadership I can recall, one

day I was sitting in my dad's 1963 Chevy, waiting for him to return from the butcher shop. We had taken a couple of deer in for butchering, and Dad was making the arrangements.

Normally we dressed our own deer out, but this year we wanted to get some sausage made. The butcher shop was on a very busy street and two dogs came out to the curb. The first was an older, unkempt mixed-breed cur, the second a younger, pure-breed Irish Setter.

Because our family hunted pheasants, we always had some sort of bird dog around the place. I was watching the setter because I thought he would bolt at any minute, risking being hit by a car.

My attention shifted to the cur, his movements seemed wrong for a dog. After watching him for a while, it dawned on me he was moving his head in a pattern that matched the traffic flow. He was looking up and down the street, waiting for all the cars to pass.

The cars just kept coming for several minutes, and the suspense was building in my mind. The traffic finally cleared, the cur gave the all is clear look to the setter. The setter fell in behind, and they crossed the street safely.

If the setter had been by himself, he probably would have been killed. The cur had fought that war of getting across the street many times. The setter had the pedigree, but the cur had the street smarts to make it another day on a busy street. I do give the setter credit for recognizing leadership when he saw it.

You only learn when you start observing the world around us. I've seen so many people that could have been saved from a lot of pain, if they had just taken the time to observe how things should be done.

A story was told to me about a culture on a remote island, where the grandparents raised the children. The parents were honored by the children, but grandparents were put on a much higher social level than parents. They worked together, parents providing the food and shelter for the family. The grandparent's job was to pass along the teachings of their ancestors to the children.

In our culture we isolate people from each other. Grandparents are separated from their grandchildren. The knowledge they've obtained in their lives is lost. In your youth, you look at the surface of the water, mistakenly thinking the wind controls the movement of the ocean. Your elders know to look deeper under the waves, understanding it is the current that controls the movement of the ocean.

Modern culture seems to believe that they have little to learn from their elders. They'll run around with cell phones in their faces, thinking it was sent from God to enlighten them. Just put the phone down and look to the elders for the answers.

The answers can come from someone like Jim or that old cur dog. You just have to prepare your mind to receive it. In my life, Martin Luther King Jr. was a man that changed this country more than anyone else I can recall. I'll never forget the words he spoke: "I have a dream that my four little children will one day live in a nation where they are judged not by the color of their skin, but by the content of their character."

His leadership is more powerful today than it was when he spoke those words. Martin's message gets stronger every year, and many of the improvements in the plight of the black culture can trace their roots back to him. His message was grounded in his faith, telling not his story, but God's message. Hateful messages of the times have dissolved over the years, but Martin's truth will always prevail.

I believe great leaders start out in their raw form as rough stones, with sensitive, caring edges. Life's events transform them into beautiful smooth gems. Would Martin Luther King Jr. have been able to understand what was needed if he hadn't been a black minister?

My guess is no. God chose him before he was born, and worked with him until he had perfected him into a masterpiece. Men assume that wealth will have some lasting value to future generations, so they pursue amassing horrific amounts of money. This wealth is supposed to give them great status, but does it really? I'll bet Bill Gates will be forgotten long before Martin Luther King Jr. is.

Then there are leaders that rule over the great nation. Presidents, generals, judges, and officials in the government have greatness all around them, but few actually obtain it. They were voted into office to be great! Sometimes the public gets it right, but more often, they are hoodwinked by clever campaign ads.

Great leaders seldom come from the elitists. Look to the underprivileged class of citizens to produce great leaders. Take someone who has had the stuffing knocked out of them. God replaced that worthless stuffing with a deeper understanding of their purpose in life.

I dislike most of all the religious leaders who spend their time preaching and practicing exclusion. They don't like those people or they damn everyone to hell that doesn't practice their style of worship.

These leaders look at a field of wildflowers with many

different colors and shapes, and judge them to be planted incorrectly. They rework the land, killing out everything except the one flower that pleases them. Not realizing diversity of the garden was God's original plan.

Insanity is only one Hitler away. Good or bad leadership will be emulated and it can multiply into a movement. It only takes a few of the right or wrong people to lead the world in either direction. I had plenty of examples of good leadership in my life.

Let me share one uncommon example of leadership I experienced. As a boy I would stay with my Aunt Margret and Uncle Hipe over the deer hunting season. Dad had to go back to the city and work until Thanksgiving.

Uncle Hipe worked as a lumberjack for many years in the wilds of Wisconsin and Minnesota. We'd sit around the wood stove after a cold day in the woods, warming our bones back up.

For entertainment he'd tell stories of his life in the woods. He told stories of wolves they'd seen along fire lanes as the made their way to the cuttings. The wolves weren't afraid of the workers. They'd sit warming themselves in the sunlight.

One cold January morning, men were moving a stack of wood for transport. They found a black bear hibernating in the wood pile. One of the lumber jacks hit it in the head with an ax, killing it.

He also told of men who were killed in the woods. One story I recalled was that when a tree was cut down it fell and hit another tree, which hit a second tree, which fell on a lumber jack, killing him.

Uncle Hipe had a scar on his pointer finger that ran all the way around the end. I asked him how he got that long scar so perfectly cut. Seems he had an infection on the bone of his finger, so he sharpened up his jack knife. He then cut all the way to the bone without taking anything for pain.

When they had time off on the weekends they'd go to a small bar where prostitutes visited. The men would drink, and then fights would break out. One such fight involved a former golden gloves fighter. He was pounding a great big Swede in the face, opening up a few small cuts and a split on his lip. The Swede finally became sick of it, picked him up and threw him across the room, breaking his ribs.

Hipe had a way of sharing his stories that kept me interested. He never talked down to me. He treated me like a man, not a kid. Back in those days, people told stories instead of being entertained by the media. The young learned from their elders in a time-honored way that's been going on for thousands of years.

Hipe and Margret had three children over the years that we hunted together. He was a big man, rough from his life spent in the woods. But when it came to his children, he was as a gentle lamb. He'd sit by the fire in a rocking chair with one of his babies on his lap, singing a lullaby until they fell to sleep. If they needed their diaper changed, he took care of business, all the while talking to them in a high pitched voice, playfully scolding them for making a mess.

He shared in the rearing of his children with Aunt Margret. His love for his children was as a natural father should be. His parenting skills were abundantly sufficient to supply the nurturing required by his children.

As the children grew, his support did not diminish. He grew into the developing role of father. If you saw him in the garden, the little ones would be following close behind like a flock of young ducks.

Hipe was a poor man without much education beyond grade school. So where did he develop the sensitivity to parent his children in such a loving way?

I believe those years of isolation in the woods, working without the love of his life, molded him into a very caring husband and father. He cherished the gift of family because he suffered loneliness in his younger years. He must have been born to be a good father, and his lifestyle finished the job.

The leadership boys require to be good fathers, doesn't have to come from their father. An uncle will do just fine. Thanks, Uncle Hipe.

When I think of modern families, where fifty percent of the children have no father in the home, it seems we are out of balance. Fathers have been replaced with boy-friends, which in many cases are temporary, providing little emotional stability to the young children.

I am glad that I lived in a world where fathers had an active role in the rearing of their children.

Parents back in my day did not expect society to do their job. They worked together to raise their children. Women expected men to be fathers, and for the most part I think they were. Women now imagine they don't need a father in their children's lives. Guess what, they got their wish. Women, of course, should be all they can be, but does that include fatherhood too? If I ask that question to a younger enlightened women, she'd probably tell me she can provide the leadership her children need. That may be true with sensitive well-educated women, but for the most part, I'd say they're 100% wrong. Usually they end up castrating their sons or stapling balls on their daughters.

Everything may go all right until the children reach puberty. Then all hell breaks loose. At this late stage, an absentee father stands little chance of asserting any leadership into the children's lives. A father's leadership needs to be supported by the mother from the child's birth until his death.

Our welfare system is structured to discourage family leadership by fathers and rewards boyfriends. Part of the problem is the women's roles in society are evolving and families cannot adjust. Woman and men need to be represented equally throughout society according to their talents, but at the end of the day the children need to have a father.

If you're a women and can't see the value of a father in your children's lives, your thinking is flawed. This flawed thinking comes from being brainwashed by our society's so-called enlightened views of family. Well, you say the guy's a bum, that he doesn't deserve his children's love. That might be true, but your children deserve their father's love, so do all that you can to make that happen.

11

PRIME MINISTER WINSTON CHURCHILL

*"Those who can win a war well can rarely make
a good peace and those who could make a
good peace would never have won the war."*

TWO YEARS AFTER I SEPARATED FROM THE service, I came down with a terrible high fever. My leg (the whole one) started to hurt, and it felt very warm to the touch.

Shi always knew before I did that I needed to see someone. We decided I'd drive myself to the VA hospital. I sat around there reading all the old magazines for a couple of hours.

I finally got to see a kid all dressed up in a pretty white coat pretending to be a doctor. This guy still had his umbilical cord attached. He didn't know what was wrong, but reassured me that I'd be all right and sent me home. He advised me to take some over the counter medications and get some rest.

When I returned home Shi said "Oh my God, you look

awful!" She called our private doctor to get me in that very day.

Our doctor examined me but he didn't have a diagnosis. He did say, "Your system is trying to tell you something is really wrong." He gave me orders to get back to the VA hospital right way. "You need some labs run." He also called the VA himself and insisted I be admitted.

So back to the VA hospital we went, only this time instead of seeing a kid, they broke down and let me see an actual doctor. He didn't know what was wrong, but he knew enough to admit me to the hospital.

They started doing the lab work required to come up with a treatment plan. After the required amount of pokes and samples, it was determined that I had a bone infection. My leg swelled up to twice its size, and green and yellow matter started running out of a hole in my ankle. I was put in isolation on an IV treatment.

After a couple of days had passed things didn't seem to me to be getting better. A nurse who was treating the wound asked me how my leg was doing. My answer was I wished they would just cut it off.

In a couple of hours the hospital sent up a head-doctor to see if I was depressed.

Of course I was depressed. Who wouldn't be? But most of all, I felt abused. The system had failed me in my hour of need.

If my family doctor hadn't insisted they admit me, I would have either been a double amputee or died from the bone infection.

Shi was pregnant with our second child. She was upset, running back and forth to the hospital. After about four days she lost our baby. I blamed the VA. It was just more collateral damage provided by the VA hospital. To my surprise, after another few days of IV treatments the leg started to change color, forming a huge abscess above the ankle.

The doctor came in to pierce it with a scalpel, and puss shot out like he had turned on a facet. That was the turning point. Within a week I was discharged from the hospital. I still have my leg to this day, no thanks to the VA hospital.

Several years later I was working for the Department of Defense. I tried to lift a heavy backup system for a computer. I knew better than to lift heavy things, but with that system it was impossible to get the people responsible for that kind of work to do anything.

I remember at the time feeling that something had just gone wrong. The next day my leg hurt, I didn't think much about it and went to work. By noon my leg hurt so badly I had to go home. I spent that night sitting up in a recliner in unbelievable pain.

I went into the VA hospital the next day. After some delay a physician's assistant saw me. He made an appointment for me to see the physical therapist. When the physical therapist examined me, he wasn't sure what was wrong.

After that, I meet with a physician's assistant who thought it was perineal nerve damage, caused by a brace I was wearing. So more delays. They made an appointment with the brace man, who ended up making me a new brace. It didn't help.

By now I couldn't walk and I'd been sitting in a wheel chair for a month. I finally had enough; I talked to a friend named Chuck, who was a physician's assistant at the VA hospital. He must have said something to them because the next day they shipped me off to a larger VA hospital associated with the Madison University system.

The following morning a bunch of kid doctors were making the rounds. A young gal reached down, picked up my leg and let it drop. She asked me how my back felt. I said it was fine. They looked some more and asked me again how my back felt.

By then, I was getting perturbed. So I asked, "Why do you keep asking me about my back?"

Her answer was, "I think you have a ruptured disk."

She was right and it took only minutes to make the diagnosis.

I thanked her, and the very next day I went to Mayo Clinic to have an operation on my back. By this time, I had lost all confidence in the VA hospital to provide good health care. Because of the delay in surgery, I have permanent nerve damage running down my leg and I've never been able to walk as well since.

Many VA hospitals will dress a monkey in a white coat and call him or her a health care provider. They're big on putting people in positions that are making medical diagnoses beyond their knowledge level.

This practice results in unnecessary suffering or death for the veterans. A lot that goes on in the VA system is more about the employees than about the patients. People are rotating through the system to get enough credit's to master some degree or have become so disillusioned that they are zombie-like caregivers. They are capable of doing a good job only on a full moon.

When you go to school to become a doctor, first you

read the book, then you slice and dice animal parts. The poor veterans are next on the food chain. The relationship between the medical colleges and veterans' hospitals seems awfully cozy to me.

This country slaughters its young lambs in senseless wars. They are used like guinea pigs to train young doctors for the private sector. The VA needs to be honest in assessing their ability to care for patients. The private sector is constantly fixing their mistakes.

In the discipline of yoga, you would call their actions a sense of the false self. Being truthful would set them free.

When problems become too big to hide, a congressman might get involved. Undeserving parasites are constantly whining to them, and they become desensitized to the voices. The whining doesn't stop with the veterans. The federal employees have strong unions, EEO. If a manager wants to fire someone, it takes a medical error the size of the Grand Canyon to get it done. Professional medical personnel have an obligation to police themselves.

In the private sector people are fired or sued for not doing their job correctly. In the VA, employees are rewarded better than the private sector without really shouldering the burden of caring for the veterans.

My suggestion is to cancel all the VA workers' health insurance, require that they and their loved ones only use the VA hospitals. If the care is good enough for the veterans, it should be good enough for the employees' children.

Presently the attitude is that care is good enough for who it's for. After all, most of the patients are poor people. When VA employees think about it, these guys are lucky to be getting any care at all. Isn't that the attitude VA employees really have about who they care for? If they had to put up with some medical student working on their children, things would get cleaned up. As a matter of fact, as long as we are adding patients to the VA role, why not add our senators, congressmen, and their family members also? So stop lying to yourself. The truth will set you free.

Some years ago the Veterans hospital in my area came up with a person to manage pain. I didn't know her back ground, but I'd guess she was a physician's assistant. Of course, she could have been a nurse, required to watch 20 hours of video on pain.

I'd been having problems with my back and stump pain. I was hurting, so my thinking was flawed. You know, having one of those brain cramps.

I checked with the Veterans hospital to see if they could help. I got a consult with Ms. Pain Queen, who interviewed me.

She had to determine what kind of pain it was. Was it shooting, stabbing, or dull pain? And how many smiley faces would I put on it? Then the queen prescribed oxy-codone, which I had never heard of, but I figured what the heck, it's worth a try.

I started taking the drug and the side effects were unbelievable. I was dizzy and my stomach was upset. I was throwing up, and I couldn't go to the bathroom. I could take a trip without ever leaving the farm, kind of half-high all the time.

I gave the Pain Queen a call, and she reassured me that after some time things would get better, that my body needed time to adjust to the new drug.

So I tried it again, only to come up with the same results. So without telling her, I stopped taking it. I did a little research on my own, found out this drug was very powerful and shouldn't be handed out like candy at Halloween. It was also addictive, and people were having problems getting off it.

Kids were stealing it to get a buzz and selling it on the street. It didn't seem to make any sense that the Veterans hospital was giving it to veterans for long-term control of pain. Clearly, one of the VA's dumber moves was having a Pain Queen controlling such powerful drugs without considering the downside. To prescribe such a powerful drug was crazy.

The first rule of medicine is to do no harm, which means a caregiver doesn't solve one problem only to create a larger one. If you have a hangnail on your finger, the doc doesn't amputate the finger to reduce the pain.

I never really followed the progression of the Pain Queen but I believe the VA now has a whole clinic handing out drugs to veterans. Disbursing drugs should only be done by your attending physician, or, in the correct setting, physician assistants, but then only if properly monitored by a doctor.

Even under the best circumstances, medications are over used. Many times a doctor prescribes drugs to get the patient out the door. They can't get rich taking the time to find out what the patient really needs. Most of the time the patient needs to take responsibility for causing the condition in the first place. Of course our country lives in denial, expecting the healthcare system to fix what we work full time screwing up.

The VA hospital along with the private healthcare system continued down this path of over-prescribing medications by doctors for years. They have now written a prescription for every man, woman, child, and most of our pets. Many lives have been shortened or severely altered with a negative outcome because the healthcare providers got rich along with the drug companies over prescribing drugs.

They actually killed some veterans, and a few VA doctors had to fall on their sword over it. I'm sure many more veterans were killed over the years, but it was never reported.

Sometimes pain is the best medicine. It informs the person they must change their lifestyle to get rid of it. How many beautiful people will have to die before someone puts a stop to this insanity?

I have one more story to share about the VA hospital. I'll call it the Grant Princess Pig.

As an amputee, I qualify for a special grant to make my home more accessible for my wheel chair. I can't just show up at the VA without a leg and they give me the money. It requires justifying the need for the grant to be issued.

So I start working my way through the paperwork to get all my ducks in a line. I did the drawings of the home, contacted the doctor to write a consult to the physical therapist, got three bids from contractors for the job, prepared a bill of materiel, and filled out all the forms. I pride myself on detail, and I put together a packet that even a monkey could follow.

What's next? I thought.

I put together a nice cover letter to introduce myself, then sent off my packet to the VA hospital grant coordinator. I was excited about doing some upgrades to my home.

A month went by and I hadn't heard a thing, so I give

the grant coordinator a call only to get an answering machine. I left her a message.

Another week went by without a return call. So I made many more calls to her answering machine. I wondered, Wow, what's going on with the coordinator?

I gave the patient advocate a call to see if he could get someone to call me, but still no calls.

So I wrote a letter to my congressman and he contacted the VA.

The Grant Coordinator finally called and told my wife I'd have to wait for one year because of a small problem of securing the property.

It is said that you can't push an elephant, especially a government grant coordinator elephant, no matter how hard you try. You must get a handful of peanuts and lead it around.

What the princess wanted was to put me in my place. After all she was the elephant. I was the veteran with too small of a bag of peanuts.

I was thinking of ways to get even with her, so I came up with the pet name for her. I call her the Grant Princess Pig. I'm unsure why anyone would want to treat a veteran trying to remain independent in such a disrespectful manner. The pig couldn't have made it harder for me to get a small grant if she'd tried.

Then there was the fact that by keeping me in my home, it saves the nation 10 times the value of the grant each year. It's very apparent she didn't have the educational background to manage the grant coordinator position correctly.

Ms. Grant Princess Pig hasn't the foggiest understanding of the human condition she is dealing with.

She is dealing with men who have been beaten up by life for years, and all they're asking for is a little help to get around their own home. They're patriots. They'd defend this country from their wheelchairs.

Sensitive, educated professionals do not conduct their affairs in such a callous, uncaring manner. Senior management turns a blind eye to problems that are very fixable because of their inability to lead. The question federal employees need to ask themselves is, Who am I here to serve?

If it's your God, country, and then the veterans, you've made the right career choice. If your answer is yourself, you're a predator.

In nature when an animal is lame, predators will gather for a meal. At the VA hospitals the same is true. Predators gather to feed off the disabled vets. I just wish they would mark the predators in some way, make them wear a special uniform or something.

I've got it. You know the caduceus, the staff with snakes wrapped around it that symbolizes a medical person? Well, instead of a caduceus they could come up with a special pin worn by people like Ms. Grant Princess Pig. It would depict a disabled veteran with a vulture circling above, ready to pick the bones clean.

I feel sorry for the VA staff that does care about the veterans, for to work with a bunch of bone pickers every day must be demoralizing. Of course, the real answer is for the government to clean house and fire the unqualified vultures. Ms. Grant Princess Pig has responsibilities beyond her circle of understanding. The truth would set her free.

It's been my experience that every time I need some

help from the VA hospital, I have to take on the role of senior management. Frankly, I'm tired of doing their job. I promise no more VA hospital stories. They're bad for my karma.

My late mother-in-law worked hard in a factory for many years, putting food on the table for three kids. She was there in body, but she had a dream of being in her own business.

Mom was sick of standing at a machine making so many pieces per hour. The job was timed so close that if she sneezed, she'd fall behind. When she was around 50 years old and the kids were raised, the time finally came for her to get out on her own.

She quit that sorry job and started her own business. She traveled around selling homemade lemonade, fudge, and art at social events. I remember her telling me that she felt like she had been released from prison. She continued to work for 15 years making her lemonade. I believe those were the happiest days in her working life.

She never got rich, but she made a respectable living for herself. She fulfilled her lifelong dream of proving to herself that yes, she could do it her way. I'm so glad Mom had those years.

Then one day she developed a terrible skin problem on her hands. After going to the doctor, it was determined that she had developed an allergic reaction to lemons. We couldn't believe after all those years of working with the lemons that she developed an allergic reaction to them.

I now understand how it happened. It's like going to the VA hospital, being treated poorly by employees like Ms. Grant Princess Pig. I eventually developed a lemon allergy to the VA hospital.

I would suggest anyone dealing with the VA hospital take a course in anger management. Instead of becoming victimized by the system, a person could learn how to cope with federal employees with mad cow disease.

Figure out a way to put lipstick on that pig. Doll her up with cowgirl boots and a red dress with a white ruffle around the bottom. Take her to the local watering trough where she can drink beer and line dance until she wears herself down.

When you get her in the mood, respectfully request to have the conservation about why you came to the VA hospital for help. Remember, this quote by Mark Twain: "Anger is an acid that can do more harm to the vessel in which it is stored than to anything on which it is poured."

It also would be helpful to watch old shows of The Three Stooges or listen to Pink Floyd sing "Comfortably Numb": "Hello? Is there anybody in there? / Just nod if you can hear me. / Is there anyone at home? / ... / I have become comfortably numb".

12

ACTOR CLINT EASTWOOD

*"The guys who won World War II and that whole
generation has disappeared and now
we have a bunch of teenage twits."*

O F COURSE, PEOPLE GIVE YOU A LOT OF CRAP when you're a vet. You know they have their head up their butt on some issues and feel the need to blame you for their problems.

I worked for the private industry first in my career, then later for the government. Coworkers in private industry for the most part were supportive of my efforts to work. In government employment, I was accused of being a double dipper. Someone wanted a job, and of course I was the reason they couldn't get one.

Well, any group of people who receive special consideration for work or other benefits are going to hear it. So I tell them that being a Vietnam veteran, I did nothing right while I was in the war, have done nothing right since I've been home, and I personally pledge to do nothing right for the rest of my life. Now I can't wait to get to Heaven because I have heard there are no assholes there blaming me for their missed opportunities.

Another big issue is your pension amount. People seem to think it's okay to ask someone how much money they get. It can put you in an uncomfortable position, so what you need to do is return the favor. The answer goes something like this: "Being disabled is a 24/7 condition, so the pay is far below minimum wage."

If they still want to know, tell them that disabled folks are paid by the length of the emotional scars that society gives them.

If none of that works, lie about your income. Tell them you get far less than they do, anything to get them off your income. What right thinking person wants to discuss their finances in public?

Many guys who didn't go to war, or went but didn't see any action, also will have a problem with the fact that you did. They would like to share in the spotlight and can treat you badly. In their minds you're hogging all that hero stuff.

Most of the time they're easy to handle with just a few words, like "all gave some, some gave all," and thank them for their service to the country. Put all the attention on their contributions, making them feel better than you. If you have any awards for heroism, don't mention them.

In my case having a leg off got a lot of attention so when asked, I just give a brief summary of events redirecting the conversation back to them as soon as possible. Never ever brag about anything you did in the war. It will only open you up for hurtful comments from whomever you're talking to.

Make them think you're the omega dog, keeping your tail down, exposing your vulnerable parts. Soon they'll take on the alpha role and you can go on to something more interesting to talk about.

Of course you can get caught lying.

One day I was standing in a line at Walmart waiting to pick up some pills. Some old lady cut the line in front of me. I was thinking Boy, what a rude person. But I remained cool, didn't show any reaction to her. I was standing alongside a bench they had for elderly to sit down, and a hatie sat down beside me.

He must have seen me limp, and he asked if I'd been in the Vietnam War.

"Nope," I replied. "Never served in the military."

I thanked him for his service, and he started telling me how when he came back people wouldn't sit by him or talk to him on the plane that carried him home from the war.

I thought this was probably a story he'd developed to entertain the public, but at least it wasn't the spitting-on-him story I usually hear.

I asked him what outfit he served with in Vietnam. He did not remember who he'd served with. Wow, that was very strange. Well, another hatie walked up and joined the conservation, only his hat displayed the fact that he was a Korean War Veteran. He told us that they were the forgotten war heroes, so I thanked him for his service to our country.

He asked, "What war were you in?"

I replied, "Never served in the military."

My older brother walks up and joins the conversation.

One of the haties asked if he'd served in the military.

He replied, "No," then pointed at me and said, "That guy right there lost a leg in the Vietnam War."

Just then I was called by the clerk to pick up my order. I was so happy I could have kissed her. I was busted by my brother, in front of these hatie heroes.

In my view, the biggest hero was the young woman handing out prescriptions for Walmart.

In my imagination, she gets up at 5:30 a.m. in the morning, looks through her underwear drawer to find a pair of panties without holes. She takes a shower and dries her hair.

On the way to fix breakfast, she wakes the kids and lets the dog out. While the kids are eating breakfast she finishes dressing, finding a comfortable pair of shoes for the day. It's time to feed the dog, stack the dishes in the dishwasher, comb the kids' hair and gives them a final inspection.

Then it's out the door to drop the kids at Grandma's house to wait for the bus. She dispenses hugs and kisses and instructions for after school. She arrives at work with 10 minutes to spare. Checks her cell phone for messages from her ex-husband, who's late on the support check. Then she rushes over to the pharmacy counter and logs into her cash register.

Now that's my description of a real American hero.

Shi and I were at a DAV function, which I seldom attend. Anyway we were setting across from a nice old couple. The speaker asks all who have a purple heart to raise their hands.

Without thinking, I did.

In less than a minute, the lady sitting across from me asked, "Are you rated 100 percent?"

I responded, "Why do you ask?"

She replied, "My husband has two purple hearts, volunteered in the Marines, and only gets a 70% pension."

What's my response? I said, "I'll see your purple hearts and raise you one bronze star."

Maybe I should have told her that I was never any good at killing people. To this day, I'm not worth a shit at it. I was a victim of the war, not a hero like her husband.

I couldn't tell her what I was really thinking. That there are those who use the system, and there are those who are used by the system. I have tons of respect for the Marine Corps. Many have served with honor. They are the heroes of the wars, a job I never wanted or felt qualified to do.

Her husband asked me years later if I would consider riding on the Purple Heart wagon they pull in the 4th of July parade.

I declined. I didn't want to steal any thunder from those Marines. They deserve the recognition much more than I.

I didn't think she could get her head around my point of view. After all, she was the self-appointed protector of fairness. Her understanding of truth was very limited and I saw no reason to try to enlighten her. Just another unthinking nice old lady using me to vent her grievance with the Veterans Health Administrations rating system.

I gave her comments a little consideration, but I don't answer her. Instead I redirected the conversation to be about him, blaming the government for not taking better care of him.

She took the bait and started in on giving the government hell. So lying or not telling the whole story is okay in the right circumstances.

What I needed to do is make her feel listened to without allowing her to draw me into a conversation about who gets what. After the appropriate time of listening to her vent, my wife and I excused ourselves.

She needed a sounding board, but we needed to get away from her to salvage a little enjoyment of our night out.

Issues like disabled parking can get some people going. Some old lady has had a knee replacement operation and thinks she is disabled. They are incapable of understanding that the whole world does not revolve around them. After all, they have been disabled for fifteen minutes and the world had better understand that makes them special.

I shouldn't be so hard on them, I have a PhD in suffering and they haven't even gotten out of kindergarten. Most of these folks can walk just fine; their only problem is that they're spoiled rotten by our medical system.

I remember this really lovely guy I met a few years ago named Bob, who was in a wheelchair for the rest of his life. A few weeks later, we were coming out of the performing arts center. I looked way out in the middle of the parking lot and saw his wife having a heck of a time getting him into his handicapped van. Well, not one of those ladies with knee replacements had any problem getting into their cars.

In my wife's younger days she made up signs, which she put on the cars she felt shouldn't be parked in handicapped parking. It gave her the feeling of straightening out the world. Kudos to her. I just park where Bob parks. Thank God I can still walk the distance.

The government is sensitive to the disabled citizen, but doctors are in charge of approving disabled parking permits. They're in the business of accommodating patients, without considering the impact on the larger disabled community. What they need to do is tell them that ignorance does not make them a disabled person or maybe it does. The really pathetic thing is that these old women or men expect society to accommodate their needs. By abusing handicapped parking, they show no consideration for the truly handicapped citizens of our nation. Disabled parking is like all the rest of the programs the government runs. They start out with good intensions and are ruined by the wannabees.

If you're denied a disabled parking space by a wannabe, first have pity for them, because they do not know they are killing themselves with laziness. Thank God for giving you the patience to deal with them.

Next, rejoice in your walk or ride across the parking lot. Knowing that this will build endurance and independence in your life. I don't mean you should pretend to rejoice, I mean you should truly rejoice. Smile, clap your hands, and sing. When you get to that store, you're going to be so damn happy everyone's going to be jealous of you. Oh, you see the wannabee looking moody; too bad she hasn't your upbeat attitude.

There is that person who is so irresponsible that society has to take care of them. They find some way of faking a disability, thinking that milking the system is the way to happiest. Most of them have miserable lives, living in an emotional poverty that consumes their very souls.

People lump the deserving disabled person in with the wannabees. That makes it hard to separate the fly shit from the pepper. Lawyers, by representing these fly shits, make it almost impossible for officials to fairly distribute social programs.

"Whose fault is it that you're disabled?" comes into the picture. "Is it your fault? Did you smoke, drink, drive too fast, have sex with the wrong person?" People want to assign blame to you for the problem or maybe blame God.

To this you tell them, I wanted to become disabled so I went to war hoping I'd become disabled for the rest of my life. I now thank God every day that I'm disabled. I'll pray that you too can become disabled, because we get a big pension, job preference, and don't forget, disabled parking.

A friend came back from Vietnam with a leg off and needed some help getting a job. He tested for a job at the post office and did well enough to get in.

Right from the start the employees were on his case about getting job preference. They were verbally abusing him, calling him a double dipper and isolating him. Seems they were upset about him getting job preference. It took a few years of this abuse, but he was finally driven out by a bunch of ignorant, insensitive employees.

Why did management allow this to go on? Shouldn't someone have been intelligent enough to put a stop to it? The sad thing is that he never worked again, because a few extremely ignorant employees weren't managed. He was trying to cope with a major disability, but all they could see is the fact that he had been given some compensation for it.

Well golly, doesn't it just make you want to go out and amputate your leg so you can get a job at the post office?

What he needed to do right from the start was have them bring it on. Get in their face and tell them that he deserved this job. Let them know that, under no circumstances, was he going to put up with their crap. He didn't realize that he wasn't done fighting the war, that his most important battle was still ahead of him.

The fact that he went to war, sacrificed his leg and received compensation for his losses was all the idiots needed. The jobs were so important to the wannabees that they felt the need to gang up on a young veteran to destroy him. He needed to treat them as hostiles because actually, they really were trying to kill him off.

Those people should have been the ones leaving. It doesn't of course stop with the post office. It goes on in every walk of a disabled veteran's life. For every benefit you receive, someone will have a problem. They'll turn green with envy if you make anything of your life. They'd much rather you were a homeless loser, begging for a handout.

That would give them the fix they need to keep their egos in good shape at your expense. So our culture plays head games with anyone receiving help from the taxpayers. To survive, you need to understand what the game is and how to master it.

People come up with some half-baked idea that no one deserves to receive any help. They believe that if the poor or the crippled would just want to work, a job would appear.

To that I say, "What planet do you live on?" The facts don't support their assertions. Many well-educated able-bodied people can't find a job in their chosen field. When I have a conversation with the able-bodied folks— you know the type, they had a silver spoon in their mouth since birth, the really big thinkers—it goes like this: they believe only qualified people should get the jobs, unqualified disabled people shouldn't get any preference.

Wow, I wonder how long it took them to come up with such an enlightened view of the world. Of course qualified people should get the jobs. Listen carefully, humans connect with other humans by their labor. Your qualifications were a gift from God, your parents, and many caring teachers.

To understand my point you'd have to be able to think outside yourself. Sitting on your high horse, it must be hard to relate to everyday folks riding a donkey. Careful you might fall, heaven forbid, you'd become disabled. Of course, I know you wouldn't expect society to make considerations if you became disabled, would you? Besides, all we see from our vantage point is a horse's ass. The world's wealth is in its work force. Can we find ways of sharing these rewards with all people on planet Earth?

If you wanted to fight our country's wars, why did they draft me? I saw very few overly qualified people fighting alongside of me in Vietnam. They were all too busy getting their spoons polished by some college to fight for the country.

After the smoke has cleared and the bullets stopped flying, they appear like flies around a fresh cow pie for any government job. You'd think they'd come to an understanding that their small minds would awaken from their self-centered view of the world. Instead they run over the disabled on their way to the front of the job line. After all, life is about only them.

I have the answer. Why not just draft only overly qualified people to fight the wars in the first place? Then they would be the ones crippled. They wouldn't need any help, because they are the most qualified person for the job. The truth is, these bastards use the poor of the nation to do the killing for them. After the war, they want them to disappear.

Nowadays we don't draft people and it's an all-volunteer force. The youth of the ghettos can either sell drugs or join the service. The poor boys down in Kentucky can either mine coal or join the service.

So when these boys get wounded, they will not have the problems the unqualified scum of the earth draftees had. I'm so glad the country fixed that problem. I know this draftee was thankful the government gave me the help I needed to join the work force.

I saw an episode of 60 Minutes where a fire department took a retarded gentlemen under their wing. They treated him like family, feeding him, ironing his clothing, helping him wherever he needed. What a gift they provided for the gentleman. Just to be supported by them was enough to make him happy. He felt loved. Then think of the example the guys are setting for their children and the community.

Citizens who have differences need to be integrated into society, not isolated, because we all have one thing in common; we want to be included in society.

In the movie The Elephant Man, the setting was 19th century London. John Merrick, the lead character, was a horribly disfigured person. When people saw him, they would recoil or scream names at him.

He was exploited by an operator of a freak show and wore a bag over his head when in public. Finally, he was rescued by a doctor, and even the queen got involved in his well-being.

There was a scene where an angry mob had him cornered. He spoke the lines "I am not an elephant! I am not an animal! I am a human being! I am a man!"

This movie was about a man who lived in 19th century London, but it could have been about the postal workers in the 1970s. "I am not a double dipper! I am not the reason you don't have a job! I am one of your own! I am a veteran who cares enough about this country to keep it safe for your family!

Folks don't have the foggiest idea how life works. They see a veteran receiving earned benefits, but forget it came at a hell of a price for many. To this day, I would give up all of the benefits I received if I could just get out of bed tomorrow morning and take a walk with my wife. To be released from the chains that have restricted me most of my adult life would be the greatest benefit in the world.

Wannabees, you seriously don't understand what a gift veterans have given you.

13

SECRETARY OF STATE
HENRY KISSINGER

"America has fought five wars since 1945 and has gained its objectives in only one of them, the Gulf War."

I WAS AT THE HARDWARE STORE, WHICH IS JUST about the only store I really love to shop at, shopping for one of my many projects. I had been having trouble with my prosthetic so I wasn't wearing it.

In comes this mother with two little ones.

The five year old spotted me, dropped his toy, and said as loud as he could, "Look, Mommy, that man only has one leg!"

Then his sister, who was a little younger, took a look my way and asked, "What happened to your leg?"

The mother is trying to get her hands around both of their mouths. She was terribly embarrassed and turning red.

The same question kept coming out of their mouths. The mother didn't have the answer they wanted to hear.

I tried to reassure her that it was all right. I understood that children say what they feel and haven't developed the social skills to monitor themselves.

So what is the right response to that situation? I've had it happen over and over in my lifetime.

When I deal with children I use age appropriate responses like, "It's all right that I have one leg," or "Some people only have one leg." If you repeat it a few times it will be all that is needed to satisfy their curiosity, or it will give the parents time to redirect them.

Adults are another matter. Most of them will hide behind the candy rack to sneak a look at me.

Well, that is to be expected. After all, you don't get a free freak show like this every day. Then, there is that person who just can't stop themselves from asking you, "How did you lose your leg?"

I have told them on occasion "I was born this way" just to keep it brief. After all, it's not really lying. You can be born again. But I usually confess to being a veteran. Then we have to discuss the war, how they thought it was wrong and they thank me for my service when all I wanted was to buy some picture hardware for my wife's honey-do list.

I wish people could just look at me, not my amputation. I wish they'd think to themselves, "That guy certainly could afford to lose a few pounds" and "What's with those old holey pants?" People wouldn't think of asking an overweight person how they got fat or a woman with one breast how it happened.

I was talking with a friend whose wife was in a wheelchair. On Sunday they had gone to church, and she wanted to sit together in the pew with her husband.

The church ladies were buzzing around insisting that she could just sit in her wheelchair for the service. His wife ended up breaking down and crying over it. They didn't understand that she wanted to get out of the chair and sit in a normal pew. She didn't want be the center of attention for an hour or she wanted to just feel her husband's body next to hers. She was bed-ridden for many years, and finally went to be with the Lord. I've always admired her husband for being such a devoted soulmate to her.

My sister, who was really overweight, had to go into the hospital for an operation. The staff had trouble handling her because of her size. They ended up putting her into an oversized bed. When I went to see how she was doing, she cried over being in that oversized bed, not over the surgery she'd just had.

People who have differences want to be treated like everybody else. When you just look at the disability, you miss the person. I know a lady, a very attractive, intelligent person, who lost her leg in her fifties. She lives in a community with fitness centers.

I was talking to a mutual friend, and asked if she swims or works out at the centers.

"No," he replied, "Because her biggest fear is that people will stare, which would make her feel embarrassed." So she suffers from isolating herself from society, being like the Hunchback of Notre Dame, only coming out fully dressed at night.

The emotional effect of an amputation can be as disabling as the physical. Intellectual intelligence isn't what you need to develop. It's your emotional intelligence that will serve you in most cases. I've known women who have been on every diet known to man, yet to this day, have a weight problem. They know intellectually how to lose weight, but lack the emotional knowledge to keep it off.

People for the most part do not know how to deal with those who have disabilities. Don't go through your life trying to educate them. Just use the appropriate response and move on. There are too many of those suckers to deal with.

Of course this doesn't limit itself to just people with disabilities. If you're black in an all-white neighborhood, you'll get similar treatment. Humans are first curious or afraid of what they aren't familiar with. If you listen to someone talking about gay people, they start out condemning or making jokes about gays in general. Next, they tell you they know this guy who is gay and is a really nice person. So once they know you, they can get beyond your differences.

It's probably way over due for the whole country to grow up to realize people have differences. That's okay. It's actually more than okay. It strengthens our nation, giving us one of the highest standards of living in the world. So parents, remember the words from the song by Crosby, Still & Nash, "Teach Your Children."

Children, when developing from adolescence to adulthood, will dye their hair red or pierce their nose so they stand out. They no longer are just one of the family, they want to be an individual. They want to be noticed, and they're trying to get attention from society. In other words, "Look at me! I've arrived! I count in the world!" This sort of behavior is understood by society because we all know for the most part, it's healthy to identify with your own generation.

I see the same type of behavior from amputees wearing shorts to expose their artificial limbs. They're saying, "Look at me. It's okay that I have an amputation. Get used to it. I have a place on this planet." They are training the lookyloos that people without legs and arms are just like all of them. Once society becomes familiar with people with disabilities, they will be able to fully embrace them as citizens. Society needs to look directly at all its citizens, not hiding any of its people away in closets. Take off those rose-colored glasses and celebrate all the beautiful people.

The Amputees Coalition of America has a program for kids. They come together from all around the nation for a summer camp. Lots of these kids are from small towns where they are always stared at by the lookyloos. In this camp, all the kids are disabled. If you're checking out my amputation, I'm checking out yours. It may be the only time in their short lives they can just be accepted as who they are and not have to deal with lookyloos. Their time can be spent building a circle of supportive friends. My guess is lots of those friendships will endure for the rest of their lives.

When I meet a child with a disability, I try not to talk about their impairment, and I don't stare at their missing limbs. I want to take in the whole child. I fight the urge to treat them any different than others. Of course, being sensitive to their needs goes without saying. I'm not treating them like they're part of a freak show, but I'm also not ignoring the fact that they may have some baggage.

Of course, people come with different needs. I find some people actually like all the attention that a disability gives them. They enjoy talking with complete strangers about their condition. You see them riding around in their cars showing off their handicapped parking permits. They seek out anyone who will have a pity party with them, giving them blow by blow details. This is a clear sign that they've allowed the disability to identify them. They've become a narrator of an organ recital.

I was chatting with a gentleman in the retirement village where I spend my winters. He began to tell me about his disability, and after about 5 minutes he stopped and said it was my turn.

I said, "What are you talking about?"

To this he replied, "In this community there is a rule; if I tell you about my disability, I have to listen to you tell me about yours." He added that he had a doctor's appointment so he would need to leave in 5 minutes.

I said, "If baring your sole helps you deal with your disability, this can be a one-way story. I'll just listen and stare at your scars while you continue your story."

Body image is formed in a person during childhood right around puberty. The awareness of what's looking back at you in the mirror is elevated in a young person's life. I believe this is especially true of women because our society over emphasizes sex. With a society so out of balance, it would be understandable that young amputated women would fear being rejected by lookyloos. This fact does not go without our Lord noticing.

One day our Creator was in his studio painting a beautiful woman. His choice for paint was water colors, because they blend well together to create soft, flowing transitions.

Looking around the studio for a canvas, he spotted a robe worn by Jesus and mounted it on a wooden cross. He began doing a sketch of her, paying special attention to give all the parts perfect symmetry.

He took a few minutes to think about how her beauty should be blended; long, blond, soft, flowing hair; deep, misty blue eyes; full, perfectly shaped breasts; and smooth, silky skin. He continued thinking until all of her features were arranged in his mind.

Studying His sketch, He realized it looked a lot like many of the paintings of women He had created over the years. Contemplating further, He realized that His image of a woman had not measured up to His ability to create beauty.

He threw the sketch in the waste paper basket and began to paint from His heart. The first thing He painted was her hair. instead of the long, blond, flowing hair, His brush mixed colors until bright red was made. Yes, that was just right, and he painted short, curly red hair. He was painting her eyes blue, but He stopped. No, blue was wrong. Green would go better with red hair. Green would also make her look more intelligent, so green it was. He thought, I have to be especially careful when forming the breasts. I don't want to get them so large they would draw too much attention to them. How about that smooth, silky, skin that's not realistic? Yes, He had it. The skin needed freckles. He painted freckles until He was satisfied. Finally He finished up all the details and stepped back to examine His masterpiece. Not bad, but something was wrong. What did He miss? It had been a long day and our Lord decided to take a nap.

He awakened in a few hours, refreshed, and studied the image of this beautiful woman. He began to laugh at Himself, seeing what His mistake was. Picking up his brush, He painted until her legs had been completely removed. Her beauty so overwhelmed Him that tears form in His eyes.

Just then, an angel came in and said, "Lord, why are

you crying?" She looked at the painting. "Are you crying because you didn't give this woman legs?"

He replied, "I've created many women with legs who are flawed in their minds. They spend most of their lives struggling with body image. It's as though they're at the circus viewing their image in a distorted mirror. When they look into a mirror, they're unsure who is looking back at them. This woman understands her beauty starts in her soul and extends throughout her body. Her missing legs will help develop her senses. Speech, hearing, touch, sight, and smell all makes her whole, not her missing legs. She can recite poetry, listen to music, be touched by a loved one, see a beautiful painting, and smell the summer rain."

The angel still looked perplexed, so the Lord continued. "As you know, I'm the shepherd with many sheep in my flock. The missing legs will allow her to help me do my work with the flawed women I created with two legs." With one puff of the Lord's breath, life was given to this beautiful woman. He commanded her to go do His work and remember that her beauty came from His hands.

Some years ago I was at an Amputee's Coalition of America meeting in Boston. A small crowd was forming in the lobby of the hotel, all looking down at something. I was curious, so I went to investigate and became one of the lookyloos myself.

When I got there, I saw a small child of not more than two years old with both legs and the left arm missing, and with just a small stump sticking out from his right shoulder. He had a very little wheelchair with electric controls, and by using his small stump was able to get around. If the child was aware of all the attention he was receiving, it wasn't obvious, and he seemed comfortable playing with his wheelchair controls. His mind hadn't developed to the point where he was worried about how others might perceive him.

Ironically Heather Mills McCartney was the guest speaker at the same meeting, speaking on how artificial legs don't have to be ugly. They had developed a line of legs that looked very attractive. Heather was concentrating on form, which is not a bad thing, but for me, function is much more important. The most attractive woman I could imagine would be one wearing athletic shorts with a carbon fiber leg running a race. Her beauty would be in her attitude. Embracing her limb loss with an attitude of "Look here folks, I might be down to my last leg, but don't count me out."

Being different is not ugly; being ugly is not embracing differences. We can't all run that race, but we all can strive to be as comfortable as that two year old child was with his body. How would a person achieve such a lofty goal? I'd suggest approaching it from the inside out. You will never educate the entire culture on what's beautiful. How about concentrating on educating yourself? If you let others control your body image, you've given too much power away. Beauty does not start at the top layer of skin. It starts before a baby is born. The mother's loving caring treatment of her own body is a root of our beauty. Every cell in your body is connected to the root; it's not possible to amputate beauty from one's body. Don't allow society to blemish God's beautiful painting of you.

14

PRESIDENT BARRACK OBAMA

"I don't oppose all wars. What I am opposed to is a dumb war. What I am opposed to is a rash war."

I WAS ASKED TO SPEAK AT MY COUSIN'S SENIOR high school civics class about my service to my country. I had a few speaking engagements in my life and was careful not to oversell the military. The last thing I wanted to do was be a mouth piece for the military. Getting some lamb slaughtered off because I had pushed military service wasn't something I wanted to deal with.

At the end of my speech, I asked the kids if they had any questions.

A young lady raised her hand. "Were you married before you became an amputee?"

The real question she was asking was, "Did your wife have a problem being married to an amputee?"

The joke goes like this: we both wear bags over our heads when making love. Her bag keeps her from seeing my amputation, and my bag keeps me from seeing her reaction if her bag falls off.

When a person is young their understanding of a relationship is very shallow, so body image is high on the list of what they want in a spouse. As you age, you're thinking matures. Most people no longer solely evaluate a possible spouse on superficial things, such as whether all the parts are there. Character, common beliefs, education, compatibility, all enter into the picture. You grow to understand that loving does not come from your sex organs, it comes from your heart. A supportive spouse is what you need. Actually, the disability can help you weed out a lot of candidates. If a perfect body is what blows their socks up, they need to be shopping in the perfect body store. I personally believe the perfect body doesn't exist. I would rather go for the perfect heart instead.

A good friend of mine came home from service with a girl waiting for him. He had a leg off, and at first she seemed all right with it. In a few months they married and things went fine for the first year. After the honeymoon period of their relationship ended, it was evident something was wrong. She was totally spoiled by her parents. His role was to continue spoiling her. At first she liked the idea of being married to a man who had served his nation. It gave her some recognition in the community.

Then the hard cold reality of living life with someone with a disability started to set in. She started to have second thoughts about the whole thing. Women usually are the first to act when things aren't right. Men know it as well, but for some reason do not want to face the problem.

So their marriage failed, because neither had realistic expectation of the other. He wanted a beauty queen, and she wanted a flawless stud to put her on a pedestal. Relationships have to be about both the partners' needs, so divorce was a good thing for both of them. They both moved on to find someone who could meet their needs.

Does a disability make you less marketable to find your life's partner? Not any more than the hundreds of other reasons relationships do not work. If you live in the wonderful world of denial and don't keep your body, heart, and mind healthy, it will. Some folks become a parent, instead of a partner in a relationship. They want the partner to act as a parent instead of a spouse. Really, that isn't an equitable arrangement. If you're disabled, you need to handle as much of the problems that come with it as possible. You owe that much to your spouse. Talk with anyone who has ever lived with an alcoholic. They will confirm what I'm telling you.

A couple I know was married for over 15 years and had a great marriage. They were good together, and I always thought they were much better people as a couple than alone. His wife was well-educated but gave up her dream to accommodate his career. Eventually I believe that is what caused the marriage to fail.

Finally they decided to get divorced. She wanted to go in a different direction in her life. He was really saddened by the loss of her. Unlike many people, instead of replacing his deep love for her with hatred, he continued to love her. They divorced not getting lawyers involved, just setting down agreeing on how to split their finances.

They had no children so it was just a matter of splitting assets. She moved away to the other side of the country, starting a life more pleasing to her desires. For the first few months there wasn't any communication, but they started to write or talk on the phone occasionally. To this day they still care for each other and cherish the years they had together.

Another couple I know married a little later in life. It

was her second marriage, his first, and she brought a son into the marriage.

Things didn't go well right from the start as there seemed to be a problem with the son and his step-dad. The husband didn't understand his role in the child's life. He was a wonderful man, but he lacked the skills to bond with the child. They had a baby together, adding more problems to the struggling relationship.

Things went from bad to worse, and it ended in a divorce. There was lots of drama in the breakup, which went on for years. They now absolutely hate each other's guts, while the daughter is singing the song (Daddy hates Momma, Momma hates Daddy, and I hate myself).

The hatred was so powerful it blinded both of them, because no one in their right mind would do that to a child on purpose. Children just want to be kids, to think kid thoughts, to do kid things, and they shouldn't be asked to carry their parent's baggage. You need to think of what impact your actions will have on the children and suck up your emotions. Don't let it run all over your children's hearts.

The reasons for relationships failing can be unfulfilled ambitions, lack of relationship skills, money, booze, drugs, adultery, and the sky is the limit here. You need to take the time to get it right. Think critically about both of your needs. Seek out people from different races, ages, and religions, folks with disabilities, folks without disabilities. Lots of people have all their parts, but lack the ability to truly love another person. These folks show up at your rodeo with bruises from last year's bad bull ride.

Why would they think that it would be okay to expect you to deal with their past partners memories? I know many divorcees who complain that all their problems are their ex-partners fault. Well really, isn't just a little bit of it, your fault? Many people I'm familiar with changed partners instead of researching their own minds for the answers they're seeking. The simple answers are, it's what you do with relationships that matters. Truly loved ones are to be treated with special care, even if you no longer live together.

We all need loving, supportive arms around us. We all need to be told we are loved. I love this quote by Anthony Robbins: "Some of the biggest challenges in relationships come from the fact that most people enter a relationship in order to get something: they're trying to find someone who's going to make them feel good. In reality, the only way a relationship will last is if you see your relationship as a place that you go to give, and not a place that you go to take."

The people that I most respect were the ones who were great spouses and parents. If they achieve nothing more than that in this world, it was enough. Those folks work hard to keep their love and respect for each other healthy. It didn't happen with fairy dust or some new age theory. It happened because they were emotionally intelligent enough to understand the value of their spouse in their life.

Shallow people with dysfunctional relationships seem to be ungrounded to me. They practice what I call flavor of the month to mask the fact that they're unfulfilled. I also know folks who seem to be most comfortable when they are alone in life, happy with their careers or content with being alone, answering to no one. Maybe they were in a relationship that was so painful that they've given up on finding a relationship that works.

I guess no one formula works for everyone. It's too easy to generalize, but try to keep your heart in a loving state. If the road you travel doesn't include another, that's just fine, but a disability shouldn't determine your marital status. The number one reason relationships fail, in my opinion is that the people are not willing to make the transition from me to us.

Years ago most people got married young, both giving up part of themselves to be born again as a married couple. That's right I said born again. You're no longer standing alone in the world. The two of you have become one. That puts demands on you and social parameters you must abide by. Isn't that a scary thing to think of, that you will be expected to conduct yourself in a civilized manner? Darn I'm stuck with what I need most, a loving supportive spouse.

15

PRESIDENT
HARRY S. TRUMAN

"We shall never be able to remove suspicion and fear as potential causes of war until communication is permitted to flow, free and open, across international boundaries."

I WAS AT MY WINTER HOME IN ARIZONA AND having trouble with my prosthetic leg falling off. I gave my prosthetist a call in February; he's in the cold tundra of Minnesota. He's a big baseball fan, so I thought I'd rub it in that I saw the Rockies play the Diamondbacks last week.

He answered on his cell phone down in Florida.

I asked, "What are you doing in Florida?"

He said, "I'm down here watching the big leaguers play in spring training."

So much for the rub! I was about 30 years old when I met Mike, my prosthetist. He was a young guy like me. I was impressed by his strong work ethic. I was having lots of problems with the old fence post I was wearing for a leg.

Back in the day, legs were made from bass wood, you felt as thou you were sitting on a fence. They had suction sockets, which meant there was nothing between you and the wood but blisters.

Mike said he could make me a new leg that actually fit. Wow, what a concept. He explained to me that the new design of the socket considers the shape of the stump. Rather than making the stump fit the socket, they made the socket fit the stump. What an idea.

I was a little skeptical, because I'd seen lots of things that didn't work out in the artificial leg business. It seems for every design that works, there are a hundred that don't.

In only a few weeks Mike delivered on his promise of a new style leg, which was entirely different than my old one. After a respectful break-in period, things started to go pretty well. This was a start of a good friendship. Mike stepped up, delivering the support I needed to keep going for the last 35 years.

Mike's business grew over the years, and he and his partners bought up almost all the prosthetic shops in my area. This was not surprising because of the way they took care of patients. The surprising thing was that it didn't change him. Many who have a little success in business develop an attitude. They start to self-destruct with women or booze, or believe they've earned the right to neglect their customers. Others will move away from their chosen body of work as they advance in their careers.

Not Mike. He wanted to be a guy who worked hands-on with amputees. He took to it, like a good pointer takes to holding a pheasant in thick cover. Mike nosed around a problem and came on point when he had an idea. He'd worked so many years helping amputees walk that he had become an amputee in his mind, a phantom walker.

I've been an amputee for almost fifty years, and I

understand what it takes to be successful. You need a strong desire to keep going, and professionals in your life like Mike to assist you in achieving ambulation. He knew the value in educating his patients, which cemented the partnership required to have a working relationship. Together we try to move care for amputees to a higher level. I would help by keeping my mind open to new equipment. We tried many ideas out for a test drive. It wasn't easy for him or me.

The trouble with advancing equipment for amputees is that there is no way of seeing if something has merit without amputees wearing it. This usually involves pain and disappointments for the people involved in the testing. Mike's work will go on after he is no longer with us, because of the time he spent building a fine organization. He has educated many new crops of prosthetists. Who knows what they will be able to accomplish in their careers? Naturals like Mike only come along once in a blue moon. If you find one in your life, you will be blessed.

The best advice I can give a new amputee is to listen carefully to what your prosthetist is saying. Are they a show dog, or are they a field dog, ready to hunt? If they're young, that's all right, you both can grow together. Some prosthetists have an ego the size of Texas, but lack the experience to back up their puffed-up self-image.

Be patient with them. Eventually maturity will let a little air out of the heads. They are really important people in your life. Do what you can to help fully develop their abilities. Young prosthetists should stay on point. Don't believe what Tom T. Hall sang about the secrets to life. Life secrets aren't faster horses, younger women, older whiskey, and more money. Prosthetist don't forget why God put you here. Mike didn't.

Caution—equipment manufacturers are always coming out with new leg parts. To see their ads, you'd think, if I had that new leg I'd be a track star. What you really need is a good prosthetist to evaluate the science. Mike and I talked a lot about new things coming to market. The amputees in those ads could walk on a broom stick. They're young and in excellent shape. On a good day, I might be able to walk around the track they're running on. I'm always interested in advancing the equipment for amputees, but equipment will never take the place of education of amputees and their prosthetist. I need to caution prosthetists too: be mindful, and don't allow equipment manufacturers to compromise your integrity. They have lots of money to splash around, which is temping in our dollar driven society.

Knowledge needs to find its way out of the deep dark places in our world. Only in the light can all of the players in this caregiving game be enlightened. I've notice lately more women getting into the prosthetics field, which will only help. After all, when you're looking for a good field dog to hunt pheasant, you don't pass up the female dogs, do you? The disabled world needs all the talent that's available to service the community.

Prosthetists are dealing with people when they are having terrible health problems. These events are life changing. I can't imagine how challenging it must be for the prosthetist. They hear the constant drum beat of poor me, why me, and me, me, me! It wouldn't hurt if you could take a few moments to give them positive strokes. When you're complaining about your leg, is it your logical brain speaking or is it your emotional pain speaking? You're in a lifelong partnership with the prosthetist, so try really hard not to dump your emotional baggage on them. Will they screw up once in a while? Well, of course you and they both will. In a shared commitment, you'll both be successful, and in isolated complaining, you'll both fail. These are special caregivers trying their best to help you walk, so treat them with respect.

Newer legs are being developed that enable amputees to run like the wind, and function wins over form every time for me. I don't care if my leg looks like a leaf spring off a '57 Chevy. Advancements in prosthetics are continuous. I try to build up my knowledge so I can separate the junk science from the good stuff. Inventors have tried many different things over the years. Maybe the materials weren't right or some part of the design was flawed. If younger prosthetists would take a fresh look at old processes, they might come up with something worthwhile.

In our country, small Mom & Pop prosthetics shops developed because at one time health care was isolated. Lately, regional centers have been buying up these small shops, forming larger companies. Like everything, some good comes from the larger footprint they exhibit. Their large size should allow for more advancement in research on a level that could bear much more fruit.

Smaller shops did not have the resources to do the research required to advance the field. Their methods of creating an artificial leg are right out of a cave man's manuals. Phantom walkers like Mike have an understanding of the interface between amputees and equipment. Knowledge needs to flow from amputees who are experiencing the problems, to people who can resolve the problems.

The last thing that I would have ever thought I would see in my life time is a double amputee, Oscar Pistorius, running in the Olympics. What most people missed, was the phantom walkers that helped Oscar cross the finish line. I was so proud of him, but equally proud of the team of professionals that assisted him on his run. Of course, he really let us down in his lifestyle choices after his success on the track. I'm not judging him. For all I know, success may have been too much for him to handle. He wouldn't be the first really talented person to self-destruct.

Events like that are game changers. Many handicapped children can now dream about competing at the highest level in the world. In the future, these children will become full partners with their caregivers to move mobility to even higher levels. There will be limitations in their lives that they should respect, but those limitations shouldn't be set by the lack of good equipment or poorly trained healthcare providers.

"Aerodynamically, the bumble bee shouldn't be able to fly, but the bumble bee doesn't know it so it goes on flying anyway" Mary Kay Ash.

Thanks Mike, for helping this bumble bee fly.

16

PRESIDENT FRANKLIN D. ROOSEVELT

*"More than an end to war, we want an end to the
beginning of all wars—yes, an end to this brutal,
inhuman and thoroughly impractical method of
settling the difference between governments."*

DURING MY LIFE'S JOURNEY, I SEARCHED FOR
the Mother of the Tree of Souls from the hellish
swamps of Vietnam to the comfortable lifestyle in the
Midwestern part of this country. The path I traveled was
slowly preparing me to be introduced to the Mother. There
is a tree that grows in the forest where all the collective
community knowledge is stored.

The forest is a very diverse environment, supporting many specimens of trees which can be mistaken for
the Tree of Souls. I explored the hills and valleys of the
great canopy that grows upon the planet, searching for
our illusive Mother. On my journey, I mistakenly identified many trees for the Tree of Souls. In time, their true
identity would be exposed and they would turn out to be
just another impostor.

As my knowledge of the forest increased, I began to recognize the trees with shallow roots could only support knowledge that grew above the earth's surface. I had a desire to experience a deeper knowledge to the wholeness of my life.

After so many years of being in an unbalanced working environment, my body decided it had enough. It rebelled, sending me into an early retirement. Once the work distractions were gone, my thoughts began to stir my soul to search for a natural resting place. I had time to explore the more remote parts of the forest.

My mind slowly cleared away the white noise that had contaminated my original thoughts. This cleansing seemed necessary for me to make room for the flow of true knowledge. Each time I ventured into the forest, the Tree of Souls whispered to me, "Come closer. Your questions will be answered if you continue your journey."

On each journey my finishing point drew me closer to Mother's hiding place. One day I was searching in a thicket of undergrowth which I'd mistakenly thought would hold her hiding place. I was tired, and I sat down on a large mossy rock. I leaned back on a red oak tree trunk. My eyelids were heavy, and they began to flutter, fighting the need for sleep. This battle went on for a few minutes, and finally I fell into a deep sleep. Rest came easily in my advanced years. A short nap would cleanse my mind of that day's built up stresses.

When I awoke, the rock had carried me to a protected hillside. I felt like a baby awakening from a nap, refreshed and ready to receive its mother's love. The tree spacing was more like a savanna than the thick forest I'd gone to sleep in.

Sitting up, I rubbed the sleep from my eyes. Was I dreaming? It took a few minutes for my senses to be fully awakened. As the sleep left me, I caught my first sighting of the Mother tree. She stood on a slope that faced the east, with lesser trees around her. She hadn't spoken to me, but my senses were telling me to come closer.

Was it my natural curiosity drawing me under the branches of the Tree of Souls or was the Mother controlling my actions? Each step that I took in her direction was easier than the one I'd just taken. I'd never been here but it felt like home for the first time in my life.

Mother was radiant, with beams of light glistening through her branches. Her long, soft branches appeared to be hair reaching to the ground. I asked, "Are the branches growing up from the ground or are they growing down from the Mother?"

They were neither supported by the trunk nor the ground, but in a peaceful harmony in their random appointed positions. The trunk's bark resembled a white paper birch tree at the base. It morphs into the color of the sky. As the sky turns gray, so do the tips of the branches.

The blossoms growing from the branches were blood red with a small border of violet. They were as big as a child's hand, with the look of an orchid. Dead center was the white stigma leading to the ovary of the flower. On closer observation their purpose didn't seem to be for the production of fruit. It was as though they were portals for some kind of connections.

The wind was gently fluttering the leaves; it was as they were basking in the sunlight. Mother's cover coat had very fine leaves that were semi-transparent. If you held them to the light, all the ribbing reveals its structure.

Grasses grew under her canopy with an occasional wildflower dispersed in an unrecognizable pattern. The backdrop of grasses gave flowers the needed space to exhibit their entire form, having the maximum impact on the landscape.

I found myself focusing on one single flower, which I knew was planted there only for me. No other soul under the tree has seen or will ever see that flower through my prism. I had searched all my life and was now ready to receive the sharing knowledge of this community. I felt overwhelmed. How in the world did I get from that thicket in the deep forest to be standing in just the right place to view this flower planted just for me?

Mother spoke. "Your journey has been difficult and I've seen you struggling for many years. It's those struggles that ready you for the gifts I'm about to give you. You could not understand my gifts without first enduring the difficult journey of your life. Come sit a while with me. Rest yourself in Mother's arms. Together, we can explore the answers to the questions you're seeking.

"My first gift to you: *Completeness isn't narrow abundance.* There is no reason to fill one's mind with endless beds of flowers. You need only find the one flower that was planted by me for you only. If one observes a bed of flowers planted too close together by human hands, the beauty of the individual bloom is diminished. When Mother plants flowers, I consider the entire landscape you are enjoying. The landscape is diverse with many plants, each adding the proper weight, to balance the environment. If the flower stood alone with no other vegetation, that would also diminish its beauty. The mixture of the community of plants is required to achieve natural beauty of the entire garden. Monocultures are mankind's plague; biodiversity should be the goal of any gardener."

While searching for a place to rest, I picked up the fragrant smells of the entire flora planted under the tree. The grasses dragged along my bare skin, leaving a tingling sensation for only a short moment. Feet not on a path made a crunching sound as they ambulated over the grasses. Small berries were being smashed as I navigated the terrain. These sounds disturbed a flock of nuthatches and they scolded me for the intrusion. When they flew off, I felt like an intruder in their world.

Mother called to me, "Come sit down on my apron. Lay your head on my bosom."

I did and felt the warm comforting pulse of her heart.

"My second gift: As *you move through this life; your actions affect the things you touch.* As you reacted to the nuthatches flying from your intrusion, didn't you feel connected to your actions? Be mindful of those connections and how they affect the world around you. Reach down and pick that ripe wild strawberry beneath your hand. Now, place it on your tongue and crush it. Now, pick a berry from the currant bush and do the same. One is sweet; the other is sour. Together they give our lives the balanced diversity intended by our Maker. In nature everything is balanced to maintain a healthy ecosystem. Humans forget they too are part of the ecosystem."

Pulling down a lock of Mother's hair, I noticed a female portal opened just above my heart. On closer observation I saw that the lock of Mother's hair I was holding was a perfect male interface. Mother whispered to me, "Make the connection."

When I plugged-in, I felt a force entering my body. It

wasn't like a thunder bolt. It was more like an awakening or expansion of one's mind. There was a connection that I was unfamiliar with. It was detecting thoughts from unknown authors searching to find a voice.

I asked Mother, "What's that connection I'm feeling?"

She answered, "It's my third gift: *Isolation is not the path to the knowledge you are seeking.* You must connect to the community's knowledge. When the mind is isolated, one can only learn by observing his surroundings. When you are communicating under the Tree of Souls, you can learn what others are observing beyond your circle of understanding. Maybe the valley you live in only grows wild strawberries, but someone else sitting beneath the Tree of Souls brings a pocket full of currants for you to taste. Humans are born with a need to connect to others. If they're in isolation, their flower's beauty will be limited."

"My fourth gift: *Knowledge is often hiding under layers of built-up protective coping skills.* Allow yourself to be vulnerable. Just be who you are, without worrying about judgment."

I did and voices began to peel away layers of prejudices that enslaved my mind. It's as if I was standing in a garden. I first saw the top of an onion sticking out of the ground. After I pulled the onion, there was dirt and protective skin to remove before I could enjoy its gifts. I now had a nicely peeled onion, but what I was searching for was a melody of vegetables.

I asked Mother, "How should I access the knowledge I'm seeking?"

She said, "You're plugged-in, so why not ask someone at the Tree of Souls if they could show you how to grow other vegetables?"

Observing others, I noticed their faces kept changing as I investigated other possible vegetables. My knowledge flowed to others, and their knowledge returned to me.

"Mother," I asked, "is this your fifth gift?"

"Yes," she replied. *"Learning requires a connectivity to others in the rawest form possible."*

Now I wondered why I haven't been able to access this knowledge all my life. I explained to Mother. "Many I talked with in my life went to the best schools, studied under great professors, but did not have the knowledge I was seeking."

Mother replied, "Great educators are needed to forge links of the chain that leads to the truth. If they haven't developed a portal to plug into, their links are isolated from Mother's chain. They cannot hear the Mother's whisperings. Their mind's receptors have not developed to receive my gifts."

"My sixth gift: *Knowledge cannot flow to you until you're ready to receive it.* In October when an acorn falls to the ground, the weather conditions are not suitable for growth. Over the winter most acorns are consumed by animals. Few survive their first season of the cold winter months. If a squirrel plants an acorn in just the right place, it will be ready to sprout when the warmth of the spring rain comes. How does that acorn know to wait for just the right spring day to launch it life? The information is stored in the Mother's oak tree roots, accessed by the generations of new seedlings that follow. If the weather remains warm late into the fall, the acorn will not sprout. It first needs to be conditioned by the changing of the seasons. Weather conditions may be exactly the same as in the spring, but life cannot begin because the acorns are not ready to receive it."

"My seventh gift: *"You are deceived by your ego, believing truth comes from one master, you.* Masters of discipline develop huge egos that serve both them and mankind. They become so specialized in one discipline that they miss the true path to knowledge. When they problem solve, much of the valuable information is dismissed. They're under an impression that all the links in the chain look like an onion. Every tree in the forest thinks it has all the information it needs to live a complete cycle of life. The information is handed down through the seeds of the parents. Along with those seeds, pests, disease, drought, and fire are also handed down. Over time the trees know how to cope with these problems. They have the benefit of their ancestors' knowledge to deal with their enemies. But what happens when an invasive threat enters the forest? If they believe that the truth only can come from one master, they will most likely perish from living in an isolated community of trees."

"My eighth gift: *Knowledge must have history associated with it to include information from beyond our short lifespans.* If you learn a new discipline in isolation, then share it with no one else, the information is lost at your death. History gives us an opportunity to build from that point of discovery forward. If we've discovered that some ideas worked well, or that they worked poorly, we can adjust our thinking to accommodate past mistakes or advancements. Keepers of the knowledge should only record the truth, not allowing themselves to be a victim of social pressure to please other authors. When sitting under the Tree of Souls we need be in the present moment, but be guided by the past."

I interrupted Mother and asked, "How is it that the

information being exchanged under the Tree of Souls has a common language? It's not of my tongue, but I understand it. I'm wondering, how could I understand a language I've never been taught?"

Mother answers, "That's my ninth gift: *higher levels of communication need to have a facilitator to capture the wholeness of the experience.* It does little good to sit under the Tree of Souls if your thoughts are not shared with others in an understandable way. The whisper must direct ideas to a laser cutting point. This action keeps the process from becoming contaminated by facts unrelated to resolving the topic of discussion.

"My final gift is balance. *Be mindful to keep your life as close as possible to a perfect balance at all times.*"

Mother sensed my mind was having trouble understanding her final lesson. She pointed to a Monarch butterfly landing on a milkweed plant in front of me. "This butterfly will leave the Midwestern part of our country in late summer and fly all the way to Mexico. There it will rest for the winter in a valley protected from harsh winter elements. In the spring, it will fly back to one of the southern states in America, lay eggs on milkweeds and die. Those eggs will become butterflies, which will travel north where they will also lay eggs and die. This process will continue four times before they arrive back here next August to start their journey over again. What you obverse next year is the 4th generation of that butterfly. When it's time for the new generation of butterflies to make the trip to Mexico, how do they know their role in the circle of life? They know because their understanding did not start at their birth or end at their death. The monarch butterfly understands all of the Mother's gifts.

"The answers to life's questions are solved with the help of many minds, some living, some unborn, and some have already gone to be with our Lord. Monarch butterflies are in perfect balance with their environment, depending on their connections with the past and future communities for continuation of the species. My gifts should be practiced in a holistic method that includes every walk of your life. Whatever subject needs clarification can be examined by the introduction to the subject matter experts in a given discipline. Principles are universally applied to the concept of community knowledge. What knowledge you are seeking matters very little."

Mother's gifts

- *Completeness isn't narrow abundance.*

- *As you move through this life, your actions affect the things you touch.*

- *Isolation is not the path to the knowledge you are seeking. You must connect to the community's knowledge.*

- *Knowledge is often hiding under layers of built-up protective coping skills.*

- *Learning requires connectivity to others in the rawest form possible.*

- *Knowledge cannot flow to you until you're ready to receive it.*

- *You are deceived by your ego. Believing truth comes from one master: you.*

- *Knowledge must have history associated with it to include information from beyond our short lifespan.*

- *Higher levels of communication need to have a facilitator to capture the wholeness of the experience.*

- *Be mindful to keep your life as close as possible to a perfect balance at all times.*

17

GENERAL
NORMAN SCHWARZKOPF

*"All you have to do is hold your first soldier who is
dying in your arms, and have that terrible futile
feeling that I can't do anything about it...
Then you understand the horror of war.*

MOTHER ASKED, "WHAT CONCERNS WOULD
you like to explore?" I thought about it for a
few moments. "Mother, using your gifts can we explore
the healthcare model for the care of amputees in this
country?" I thought Mother would rebuff such a monu-
mental endeavor. "Gladly," Mother responded, "Share
with me your observations. Tell me how you have dealt
with your health needs without including my gifts?
Please begin."

I sputtered before starting. "I've been an amputee for
almost 50 years, so getting to know how the healthcare
system operates was paramount. I'm at least aware of how
some VA hospitals operate. I'm pretty sure most private
hospitals operate very similarly. The care for amputees is
dispersed through clinics, which meet once a month or

as needed. Amputees present their healthcare issues to a group of professionals. They decide what would be the correct intervention to resolve the problem. The professionals at the Veterans hospital clinics are an administrative prosthetist, a physical therapist, sometimes a doctor, a private prosthetist, and admin or technical personnel. In the clinic, questions are asked and answered. Finally, a prescription for some sort of prosthetic equipment is ordered. The whole process can take no more than 15 minutes, and it has an assembly line feel to it."

Mother asked, "So equipment is the focus of the clinic's meeting?"

"Yes. It's all about what equipment is needed for the amputees."

Mother said, "So you feel equipment is overrated because it's easy for them to understand?"

"No," I replied. "Equipment is neither easy to understand, nor over rated. It's just how they simplify their response to a complex problem by shifting the responsibility to a prosthetist."

Mother said, "I'm confused. Please enlighten me."

I replied, "I believe a treatment plan needs to be developed for the amputee that is holistic in scope. The world they live in doesn't include a large enough view of the problem. If something doesn't work, they just provide a new piece of equipment and consider it fixed."

Mother asked, "Is the source of the clinicians' education too narrow."

"Yes, it's definitely incomplete, making it flawed."

Mother said, "We shall discuss equipment first. Different parts of a prosthesis come together to support each other's functions. Let me show you by example. What's on the end of an amputee's artificial leg? A foot, which is the platform they use to walk on. Now, what is the interface between the ground and that foot? A shoe. A shoe provides the needed stability, comfort and assistance in ambulation.

"Shoe designers already consider the end-users' challenges. Take a look at any organized sport in our country; you'll see that shoes play an important role in the athlete's ability to perform."

I said, "Yes, but when I asked an orthopedist or prosthetist what shoe I should be wearing, they don't know shoes."

Mother said, "Well, I'm saying if you don't know shoes, you don't know your job. Invite shoe manufacturers to sit with you under your Tree of Souls. Together, design the best shoe for an amputee to wear."

Then Mother asked, "Can you think of another way to address the challenges of designing an interface with the ground?"

"Yes I can. Why design the artificial foot to look like a human foot, then fit a shoe over it? Would walking be better for amputees without that interface of shoe to foot? How about making them just one piece, as you do when developing running legs? The foot could be designed to service an artificial leg. It might have joints in different places or no joints at all. There are people already designing feet to be the only interface with the ground. Why not take a serious look at what they have to offer?"

"You've opened the door for further discussions of equipment. I'll determine whether the professionals are following your thinking by asking another question: Does this observation lead you to consider other equipment?"

I said, "Hmm, how about the foot that isn't amputated? Shouldn't that platform be designed to maximize the balance, stability and comfort of the amputee?"

Mother said, "Do you see that this process will need to expand to include every piece of equipment that touches the patient's body? For now remember at this point, we don't have a shoe manufacturer sitting under the Tree of Souls when we discuss knees. We gathered all our information from equipment manufacturers. The blending of parts will be accomplished by another group of professionals familiar with kinetic energy, which is the science of motion. Equipment manufacturers' thinking is isolated to their discipline. They don't see the whole garden. When you're selecting plants for the garden you need to think biodiversity, not monocular."

Mother continued. "Another discipline I would seek help from would be educators of professional dancers and ice-skaters, and athletes from Olympic sports. They've studied the human body, and they have a deep understanding of strength, movement and balance. If the right humans examine all the links in the chain, you'll soon come to understand how to improve the weakest links. Remember, the links of the chain exist to support each other. They all attach to the weakest link, the amputee. Equipment has an end point to it, whereas knowledge has no limits.

"Shall we move on to what you really need to know to care for amputees? You now need to invite people with training in the health of humans to sit under the Tree with you. They would be from disciplines from which amputees are crying to get help. Many people have sat beneath my canopy, crying out for help, but no one came to sit with them. Can you hear a young man crying while he sits on the edge of his hospital bed after an operation to amputate his leg? He's having an emotional meltdown, thinking this cancer will come back somewhere else in his body and he'll die from it. How will he ever face his classmates, friends and family? Will they reject him? He doesn't possess the emotional skills to deal with such a huge life altering event.

Frankly, I believe most people do not. When his parents come into his room for a visit, he announces that he wished the cancer would have killed him. When actually, he was very lucky the medical profession found the cancer in time to save his life. Amputation is an emotional trip that shouldn't be taken alone. Many cry out for help, saying things like this young man is expressing. What they're really saying is they're frightened and they're grieving the loss of their leg.

"Doctors who study the mind know that grieving has many faces. Will it be the face of anger, denial, defeat or acceptance? Or some other face currently unknown to us? The medical society needs to be working with new amputees, one on one, to nurture them as you would nurture a flower in the hot house, slowly increasing the flower's exposure to the full force of the sun. When it's strong enough, they transplant it into a bed of flowers. After the flowers have established a good root system, they should require less maintenance. Of course we've all seen a bed of flowers wilt and die in a time of drought. Professionals should keep a hose around just in case it's needed. The planting bed could be the Amputees Coalition of America, or other volunteers can help carry some of the load. Professionals should know when and how to help an amputee connect his actions with changes in his life."

Ask yourself how many Americans are depressed for no reason other than being human? Depression is like the ocean waves rolling into a shoreline; as they roll in, they become more shallow. There is that point where the wave's volume runs out of space causing it to erupt vertically, rolling over on itself.

For severely handicapped citizens, those waves are bigger, washing great white sharks into the tide pools. The medical society needs to assist the handicapped citizen in harpooning these killers. Mother suggests that a mental health caregiver grasp a lock of her hair and plug-in.

I'm a fair skinned person with soft, easily damaged skin tissue. I've had pain for my entire life as an amputee because of skin breakdown. Artificial legs fit over your stump, and skin was never meant to be enclosed in a sealed container for 16 hours per day.

These conditions create a perfect storm causing various skin problems from blisters to skin shears to an array of abnormal skin conditions. No one has really come up with a way to treat these problems in a proactive treatment plan. Many create products that deal with the problems in a reactive, isolated treatment plan.

Managing skin breakdown gave me a lot of problems in my life.

"Mother who do I need to get help from to keep my skin in line?"

"Perhaps you could have a dermatologist grasp a lock of my hair and plug-in. I'm not talking about the standard rash doctor. I'm talking about a doctor who understands what effects artificial legs have on skin breakdown. I'm talking about an educator who can publish their findings. Amputees need to understand how they can improve the quality of the skin on their stumps. I suggest they might ask a mature nurse who had years of experience in treating patients who are bed ridden to sit awhile under the tree."

Folks where I come from use cast iron cookware to fix many down-home country meals. To cook with cast iron one needs to know a few things about the natural order of events. Mix water and cast iron together, you get surface rust. So when you first buy the pot, you need to season it. You do this by slicing a potato in half, and then salt the sliced portion of the potato with sea salt. Pour flaxseed oil into the pot and rub the oil into the pores of the cast iron with the potato. Now, stick the pot in the hot oven for one hour. If done correctly, the cooking of meals in the pot will keep the surface seasoned with very little maintenance.

Stumps are a lot more complicated than cast iron pots. Your body is constantly trying to bring your skin into balance, so stop fighting the process. Proper hydration of skin cells comes from the body by receiving enough water during the day. Many drinks add unwanted chemicals to the body, so consider what's mixed with the water.

Bathing is another concern. Consider how much fluid the skin cells were holding before you donned your artificial leg. Consider bathing at night, and if your skin needs any assistance for healing, treat it at that time. If you bathe at night your skin has overnight to absorb the lotion, while skin cells lose the water stored from the bath.

Some folks tell me when they bathe, they don't wash or dry their skin harshly and use only warm water. Do not sit in a bath tub or stand in a shower for more than five to ten minutes.

Still others tell me to scrub my skin harshly for a longer time to remove built-up dead skin. Who's right?

They both are. The point is, you must be able to read the condition of your skin.

Going back to my cast iron pot, different dishes will affect the surface of the pot. Occasionally you may need to retreat the pot with a little oil.

The condition of the skin on your stump will change constantly. Say you apply skin lotion on your stump at night to treat dry skin conditions. You have the impression it's absorbed into the body, and it sort of does. Really most of it just lies below the surface, waiting to be sweated out the next day. Oh, you did notice your interface wasn't as intimate the next day, kind of slip-sliding away?

You need to use all your senses to become aware of good skin health. You do it by recognizing the feedback your body provides over time. Skin care is one of the most important elements in ambulation. To be a little tongue-in-cheek, say you have a lot of skin in the game.

Another guy I sat under the Tree of Souls with happened to be my pop. My pop had his leg amputated in his later years because of a clot in his leg from diabetes. He had a leg made for him but couldn't wear it because his fitness level wasn't good enough to maintain ambulation. My family got the idea that because I could walk, Dad should be able to walk.

Pop was upset by all of them thinking he was codling himself and asked if I would take him to my prosthetist. I sat with my pop, watched him cry over it. The prosthetist, Dad, and I all sat in the prosthetist's office and agreed that pop wasn't strong enough to wear an artificial leg.

For the first time in his life, my father was unable to cope with what was happening to him.

Where does the strength come from to walk when the

muscles have been amputated? Modern prosthetic limbs have advanced science to assist the amputees in walking. Carbon fiber leafs and computerized knee systems have moved the needle in the right direction. But there still is only so much equipment can do for you.

What muscles you have left should be in excellent condition. Ambulation takes a lot of strength, and the higher the amputation the greater the effects. If you have both legs amputated, the effects on strength isn't multiplied by two; it's multiplied by fifty. A physical therapist should be able to evaluate the patient's muscles and design an exercise program. This program would not only strengthen the muscles to achieve maximum mobility, but it would also educate the amputee as to how they can walk with the least amount of effort.

Generally speaking, it's the joints that give humans problems. All the joints from the ankle, knee, hip, back, shoulders, and neck need to be in the correct alignment to maximize the body's orbit of a walk cyclical. If this can be achieved, the amputee walks with much less energy expended.

There are many other synergies derived from the proper alignment of joints. Breathing is better, and there is less wear on joints, fewer injuries, and increased blood flow to joints. When you constrict one joint it affects all the others.

One wonders what worldly good comes from fitting an amputee with an artificial leg when they lack the enlightenment required to walk with it. Mother suggests a physical therapist grasp a lock of her hair and plug-in.

I saved nutrition of the body for our final discussion. "Many years ago I was visited by a woman seeking knowledge on how to maintain her weight. She shared with me that in her early years after her amputation, weight was easier to control. As her age increased so did her weight problems. What was causing the weight to fluctuate so much?

After we sat for a spell with others under my canopy, the answer became apparent to her. It was discovered by the group that as her activity level decreased, her weight increased. Movement will always be a challenge for amputees; you just do the best you can.

Now, good nutrition is something we can achieve. Certainly you don't need legs to be a great cook. If you gain or lose 10 lbs., your stump's interface is compromised. Whales can't wear artificial legs. Also prosthetists will not successfully be able to fit an amputee whose weight is fluctuating. The changing weight and the average amount of weight needs to be controlled.

On her own the woman tried all kinds of starvation diets, losing pounds only to gain them back. Her life was a living hell, going from one problem to another. Because what's worse than being a fat amputee? Being fat, skinny, fat, skinny, and some more fat, fat, fat, and throw in a skinny.

What the medical society needed to provide was a great chef with a learned discipline on how to teach her the correct connection with the food she ate. This chef needed to teach her how to cook. First she tastes his cooking and then he tastes her cooking. In honoring the need to maintain a consistent, healthy weight, she would have reduced the number of problems and costs associated with amputation. She needed to become a student of culinary science. Working harmoniously with a professional chef would have been her way to weight control.

Did you notice I did not say a dietician, I said a chef? Dieticians have been told by educators that a balanced diet is made up of certain foods in reasonable portions. Well, doesn't that just blow your socks up to have all that useless information? If I ask a dietician to teach a dog how to roll over, they'd enter the room with a card picturing a dog rolling over. Proudly, they would say, "If you roll over, I'll give you a small bone this size. If you don't," and the dietician shuffles the pictures, "you'll look like this big fat pig on this picture."

The dog gets out her handkerchief, tears up and says, "I'm a dog, not a pig."

The dietician says, "If you keep eating like a pig, I'll make you ride around in the fat cart at Walmart."

A chef would cook something that would get the dog's attention, and cup his hand over the food so Rover could smell it but not eat it. Next he would physically grab the dog and roll it over, then feed him the treat. You see, Rover cannot understand what the dietician was showing him. It means nothing to the dog to see a picture of a healthy dog or a pig riding the fat cart.

On the other hand, the chef is speaking in dog. The dog thinks All I have to do is physically rollover, and I get a treat.

I taught my dog at home to pray, which took me a long time. Praying is very similar to begging. Except I had her cross her front paws. That was an abnormal movement for a dog, but after physically crossing her paws for a few months, she finally got it.

Now she comes and gets me while I'm killing off brain cells watching TV, asking for a treat. She comes into the room and tries to make eye contact with me.

I see her but pretend that I don't.

Her next move is to throw her head back and jump backwards.

Oh, that's so cute, so I get up and get her a treat. I've turned her into a religious fanatic who prays several times each day. I wish now she would forget that stupid trick I taught her.

Dieticians, are you getting any ideas, first I trained her to do something unnatural, then she begs me to do it several times a day?

The whole country is in trouble when it comes to dieting. If you are to be healthy, you need to totally connect with food. Know how to shop for the highest quality foods grown organically. Prepare food when it is at its highest nutritional value. Select recipes that consider what the body needs to stay healthy.

Last of all, consume the right amount of food required to stay healthy. By infusing the mind with the body, your skills will increase daily, and you'll learn to select, prepare, and plan meals that support your goals. Food shouldn't be a foreigner in the body; it needs to be part of the family.

To completely understand your family, take a look at where the food comes from. Is the meat that you consume from healthy animals, or is the produce from organic soil? The air and water, what condition things are raised in, all matter. Why? Because you are eating what your food eats.

Mother suggests, "A great chef, grasp a lock of my hair and plug in, whose teachings are the most highly valued of all the guests under my branches."

"After all these points, Mother, do you think our health-care system is even brushing the surface of effective care?"

18

AUTHOR MYRA MACPHERSON

"Above all, Vietnam was a war that asked everything of a few and nothing of most in America."

THE BIGGEST PROBLEMS WITH THE VA hospitals are their size and their corruption by special interest groups. They've become a dysfunctional body unable to maintain the necessary discipline to provide quality care. If you attempt to carry water in a large shallow dish and stop quickly, the water will spill over the front of the vessel. Now, try to carry the same water in a deep small diameter pail. If you stop quickly, not much happens. Health care is similar, it needs to be in the right vessel to be transported.

Veterans are used by politicians to get elected to office and by medical students to fulfill some requirements before advancing their careers. Of course, there are federal employees working their way to the top of the shit pile. Private companies, state government workers, or any other small-thinking organizations are allowed to dump their retired employees on the VA hospitals. They overload the system with healthcare issues that have nothing to do with military service. The DAV assists veterans in finding some medical condition with a small thread of truth linking it to their military service. Once they establish that connection they kick the manure spreader into high gear.

Well, hatie heroes if you wrap a flag around bullshit, it still smells like manure to me.

The joke goes like this: The veteran comes home drunk with his red pickup truck all smashed up. He has a big fight with his common law live in. He even kicks his favorite hunting dog around.

"Now you've made me depressed, gloom, despair, agony and pain."

She threatens to leave him and take the dog with her. "What's wrong with you?" she asks.

Not having any excuse for his actions he says, "I don't know. I've felt this way ever since I came back from the Sand war."

She thinks about it for a few minutes and comes up with a diagnoses, after all she watches Doctor Phil every day. "You must have been damaged while handing out toilet paper in the army. We need to go down and see if the VA can help us."

Now, he knows he wasn't damaged handing out toilet paper in the army, but it sounds like a story he could talk himself into believing.

"I wonder, honey, do you think they'll buy me a new red pickup truck and get counseling for the dog?"

"They should; it's their fault."

Meanwhile back at the VA hospital, they have some of their big thinkers studying the disorder. They call it Damaged While Handing Out Toilet Paper Disorder (DWHOTPD).

"Mother, I know I'm kind of over the top again with my humor."

It couldn't have anything to do with him investing all his efforts in consuming Budweiser beer, smoking pot, and an isolating lifestyle. Tell us the truth; do you have a plan to get rich saving beer cans for your retirement? Man up, change your lifestyle; stop working so hard to self-destruct. Recognize that your addictions are destroying you. I love wounded warriors and would give them the shirt off my back. I don't care if their injuries are physical or mental, they deserve excellent care. Now, I'd go along with counseling for the dog, but not a new red pickup truck!

Well-run private hospitals have caregivers that span the experience level from people right out of medical college to senior doctors ending up their career. Think about what I've just said. It takes 50 years of hiring the right people to build the correct balance of caregivers.

Now if you're at the veteran's hospital, you may see a farrier who shoed horses for the army. While doing his job he hit his thumb with a hammer and screamed a couple of swear words, spooking the horse. He threw himself on a live horseshoe, protecting his comrades from the stampeding creature. For his action, he received a Purple Heart, a Bronze Star and a job from the VA hospital. Even if he stays with the system all his life, he still is only qualified to shoe horses.

Another problem as I see it from an amputee's perspective is that the caregivers lack the understanding of the complexities of keeping people walking. They hand the care over to a private prosthetist, believing that releases them from the process. Private prosthetists are certainly the right people to make prosthetic legs. But there is so much more that needs to be done to accomplish the end goal of assisting someone in walking. The prosthetists job, as I see it, applies mostly to designing and manufacturing the right equipment for the amputee. Their discipline is interfacing manmade equipment with God made flesh and bones. They shouldn't be asked to do jobs unrelated to their field.

Ask yourself, what am I sitting in a clinic for? I'm not a prosthetist, so I must be here for reasons other than manmade equipment. I've got it; you're here for the God made flesh and bones. You have to help the amputee deliver a healthy body to the prosthetist so they can do a great job. I believe as an amputee, you have the responsibility to deliver a healthy body to the process. You know you're going to need some help.

I said, "Mother at this point, do you have any additional thoughts?"

She replied, "It's obvious the VA hospitals can't connect the dots to produce an image that you can clearly understand. Healthcare providers need to think of the origin of the medical problem, focusing on the patient before them. Presently, caregivers stare through a zoom lens of the camera. They quickly bring the picture into focus and press the shutter. What they need to do is, put the camera down and use sneaker zoom. That's where you walk up to the subject and take the picture without zooming in. When artists shoot in raw format, many pixels will be captured. Then once they edit the image, they can decide which pixels are needed to create a piece of art. Qualified caregivers need to enter the picture when needed, implementing their medical expertise in an effective manner. Steering committees need to be formed of healthcare whisperers, folks who are sensitized to the highest level possible of understanding amputee's challenges. They would be able to enlighten caregivers as to what amputees need to walk successfully for life. Healthcare whisperers are the most important people in the circle of knowledge required to improve the level of care for patients."

I asked, "Where would these healthcare whisperers come from?"

"They would come from private care and government employees. In the last few years of their careers, they would join together under the Mother's Tree of Souls and share community knowledge."

I'm actually very surprised any amputee is successful over a lifetime, given the present day dysfunctional medical culture. To address patient's health needs, caregivers need to learn to listen in a tongue that is not their own. There are many reasons cited for their failure to get it right, such as financial, time restraints, coordination of care, or blaming the patient for not taking responsibility for their condition. When the real truth is, thinking deeper about a modality of care would give them the time, money and resources to resolve problems in a larger theater. They go for the easy money with minimum thinking. Healthcare whisperers need to coordinate care through interaction with all the minds under the Tree of Souls, being a bridge between the caregivers and amputees.

Why not create a new position to run the amputees program? I'm not talking about another administrative prosthetist keeping track of the cost of artificial legs and arms. It would be a position created to coordinate all the players needed to run a successful amputee care center. Look to the physician's assistant program to develop a person with specialized training in the care of amputations. What healthcare providers really love is interventions to healthcare problems that they think can be solved with equipment or drugs. Why? Because the model is built by equipment manufacturers and drug companies. They successfully sell hospitals expensive equipment or drugs that are easily dispensed by doctors. This maximizes the hospital's profits. In medicine, time is money. The goal is to see as many patients in an hour as possible. Doctors need to keep those prescription pads flowing, and a steady line of procedures scheduled for all that expensive equipment. Neither medicine nor equipment is high on the list of important interventions professionals should be considering to help patients.

Mother thanked me for sharing my perspective of the problems I experienced, then said, "Let's review which people you think should be sitting under the Tree of Souls with you. You requested the use of healthcare whisperers/educators be explored. A new position would be created to run the amputee program. Their job would be to see that the correct medical personnel with the proper education are in the healthcare loop in a timely manner. In your view, the four biggest issues amputees face are, emotional health, skin breakdown, physical strength and controlling their weight. All these disciplines need to be practiced under the Tree of Souls. Do you know of the Three Sisters?"

"I've heard of them, are they from the Hopi Indian culture?"

Mother said, "Native Americans have grown corn, squash and beans in one connected planting plot for years. They viewed these plants as one family. Inseparable, a special gift from the Great Spirit. Each plant benefits from the other. The cornstalk supports the climbing bean vines. The beans help replenish the soil with needed nutrients. The squash provides large leaves to shade the planting plot, keeping weeds down and conserving water by reducing the ground's exposure to the sun. With this concept, they were able to successfully cultivate thousands of acres in the desert for hundreds of years. They understood to grow a garden in an environment of extreme conditions they needed to pay special attention to the care of the Sisters. With their digging sticks, they created canals to provide the plants with the life-giving water they needed."

The clouds that hold this life-giving emotional water form in the heat of the summer months. When rain does come, if the environment isn't ready to store it, little good comes from the storm. Man has so altered his natural watershed, he does not benefit from the water that rushes by. A meandering stream working its way toward the thirsty plants is what's needed. As this water kisses the plants, they become joined as one. Love between emotional health and physical intervention creates complete wellness. When wellness is born it's a small baby requiring nurturing for the rest of its life. A baby is born by a physical act and sustained by emotional love.

The wearing of an artificial leg is living in extreme conditions, so the concept is very similar as how to achieve a successful lifecycle. The difference being, our Three Sisters are the health of the skin, the fitness of the body and the weight of the body. Then of course, the amputee needs to view the care of these physical conditions, from the life-giving water of their emotional health.

What should be the first goal of the healthcare

providers? They need to learn how to use the digging sticks. This would connect the emotional water to the physical Sisters' bodies. Once the water has reached the seeds, the Three Sisters can begin to grow stronger, producing a crop. The caregivers are unable to teach because they are not aware of Mother's gifts. The system operates in isolation, and communication isn't through the Mother.

"Mother, would you please enlighten the caregivers of what needs changing?"

"Doctors and therapists know of education, but it's not given an equal weight in resolving health issues. The voice of education is only allowed to whisper with a hoarse voice. Now the voice of equipment is allowed to scream at the top of its lungs. Community knowledge includes all the voices under the tree, not just the ones screaming. They also lack the awareness to know when to use the digging sticks."

To answer this question, we need to go back to the Native Americans for clarification. Where did the birth of the Three Sisters come from? They may have dumped crops in a pile, each one of the Sisters took root. Over time the Native Americans became aware that these plants did better than all the rest of the individual plantings.

Knowing all things require water to grow, they dug canals to supply water to the Sisters. If you've ever traveled in the southwest, you understand how hot and dry conditions can become. These conditions leave the earth as hard as a rock. Would the Hopi Indians have added canals in those conditions?

Unlike our medical professionals the Indians lived in harmony with the earth. They would have waited until the rains came, leaving the dirt soft enough to create or add to existing waterways. Some of the earth might need to soak for a while before it was ready for digging.

Caregivers, this is the time to think more deeply about how you are going to improve the medical system. These Sisters are not limited to amputees. Think who else needs the emotional connection of the water? The answer is everyone.

Think of physical health and emotional health as one family. You need to sit awhile with the Mother and explore how big the family is. Caregivers, get your digging sticks ready for the rainy season. Because I'm positive no matter what crop you're cultivating, it will require the whole family to obtain a good harvest.

Society needs to plant, fertilizes and water our citizens throughout their entire lives. Could you image a teacher planting an idea in a first grader's head that they are responsible of taking care of their own health? Other teachers would fertilize and water the idea as the child grows. Our health would be a continuum from childhood to death. Think of how much easier your job would be.

Have you heard of TED talks? If you haven't, it's an organization that brings together speakers to present insightful presentations about different subjects. Is it possible to do something similar with patients?

Start with Sister Weight Control; introduce the amputees to a master chef. Create the foundation to assist amputees in weight control. Over time the amputees would learn from the chef how to prepare meals. Remember, diet will only be successful if the canal is dug for emotional water to flow. The most important element of health, the diet, could finally be addressed, giving amputees the building blocks of a successful life.

This concept could also be used by physical therapists. There are exercises and stretches necessary to maintain a good range of motion. If I do a great job in the morning of stretching out my calfs, hamstrings, and hip flexors, my gait is improved for the whole day.

Therapists, are you supplying the right digging sticks to get the water to needed joints? Don't try to dig the canal in one session. Develop programing to lengthen the canals when the earth is soft.

Does a Minister cover the whole Bible on one Sunday morning? No, he spends his life going back, retrenching that canal to keep the life-giving water flowing to the congregation. The therapist can't put what is needed in a box and ship it to the patient. They'll have to develop working relationships with their patient's, teaching and motivating amputees to rise about their disability.

Remember what I told you about using the digging stick to connect the emotional being with the physical being? This will also work for skin breakdown. If problems were broken down into categories, like bathing, skin shear, sweating, hydration, and so on, problems with skin would start to find a resting place. You could find a cure for that chapter of the skin book.

Share this information with specially trained healthcare whisperers from all over the country, establishing goals that actually address the living conditions of amputees. Patterns of effective methods of care would begin to unveil themselves. The system would begin to recognize its weaknesses and correctly change their operating systems. From that information, you could develop training programs to move the care for amputees to the highest level possible. Remember, we are dealing with the emotions, assisting in opening water gates and allowing knowledge to flow to the physical body.

If an architect is designing a home for a client, where would he start? The first thing would be to interview the clients. That would give him the information needed to design a home that fits their lifestyle.

The second thing they'd do would be to teach them that architecture has rules. These rules should be followed to achieve good harmony with Mother Earth. They'd touch on things that the untrained client never thought of, asking questions to enlighten their awareness. The client tells of their desire to have huge south-facing windows to capture the mountain view.

You explain to them that they live in Arizona, and that those windows will also capture summer heat. This will leave the house unlivable without consuming huge amounts of resources to cool the home. They complain that the reason they bought this lot in the first place was the view of the mountains. The Mother Architect knows why they bought the lot. The architect now asks permission to design a home that considers the environment it's placed in.

The bones of the home will need to be moved or perhaps have an overhanging roof system. If encouraged, the architect will design a home that meets every one of their wishes. The home will also settle into the landscape as it should.

Most healthcare providers build their patient's houses with huge southern-facing windows and decks. The patient fights the exposure to the sun all their lives. If you're looking to build a healthy lifestyle, don't hand over your medical condition to someone who only knows how to build tract homes.

"Every human being is the author of his own health or disease." — Buddha.

To be a healthy person, you need to work hard to practice discipline. If you cannot whistle then you cannot walk, because your first steps are in your mind. You will have problems dealing with your health; it's a matter of when, not if. That is why you need to listen to the Mother, sit under the Tree of Souls with her. Try to build a supporting circle of professional caregivers that are at least willing to listen to our Mother. You can handle the challenges of walking with an artificial leg. There's no reason to sit in a wheelchair for the rest of your life.

My point is, if you can walk, please do! I know from experience, people wearing an artificial leg have a higher quality of life. Mobility comes at a cost, but sitting in a wheel chair for the rest of your life also comes at a cost. If you don't carry your end of the log, you will not walk. If you attempt to master any discipline, you'll need to work hard at it.

My words are harsh on the caregivers serving the amputee community, I'm not being disrespectful. I'm trying to raise their awareness, to consider the knowledge of the community. We really need to have a tremendous amount of respect for special caregivers, devoting their lives to the care of amputees. That's why I've introduced them to Mother.

19

NEWS ANCHOR
WALTER CRONKITE

*"I covered the Vietnam War. I remember the lies
that were told, the lives that were lost—and the
shock when, twenty years after the war ended,
former Defense Secretary Robert S. McNamara
admitted he knew it was a mistake all along."*

M Y DEAR TEACHERS, DO YOU THINK THAT
the playing of sports has something to do
with a healthy nation? The truth is, educators teaching
a sport do almost nothing to improve children's
health. Schools spend enormous amounts of resources
teaching students how to put a few points on a score-
board. They should spend their resources wrapping
their arms around the families of the students in the
classrooms. Giving them the emotional water they
need to stay healthy. They will become kinder, gentler,
healthy families.

In the animated film Avatar, the hero of the film had
to ride a great flying dragon. The first thing he needed to

do was make a connection between their spirits. Once he accomplished the connection, he and the dragon became an awesome fighting machine.

Educators, you also need to make that connection with the great flying dragon just outside the classroom. Education is a community activity, not to be practiced in isolation. Families isolated from the herd are killed off by the wolves. It's going to be so thrilling for you and the families when the students ride the great flying dragon.

Students sitting at the foot of the Tree of Souls, request that everyone in the circle honor your life by sharing in helping you obtain your goals. Ask them to pull down a soft branch, insert it into their portal. Knowledge can now flow between each one connected to you. That knowledge is no longer isolated. It is now shared intelligence in a community setting.

This connection will lead to the success of every one's life sitting under the Tree of Souls. Did you ever wonder what people did before healthcare systems existed? They shared what knowledge was available with each other through their mothers. Will caregivers continue down a path that leads to tomorrow's problems? Students, next time you see your teachers, asks this question. Would you teach me to ride the dragon?

I have another story to help you understand the meaning of these lessons I profess to be the truth. My grandson, Tate, tried out for a part in a play, Mary Poppins, and was picked for one of the leading roles. We got word that Saint Mary's College in Winona, MN was performing the same play. Our grandson needed to do research, so we took him to the play.

This play had many actors in it. As the play opened, I
noticed a young man with Down's syndrome was an actor
on stage. As the play continued, there were more physically and mentally handicapped actors on stage. In all, the
number had reached, maybe, twenty percent of the cast. I
thought this director certainly was an enlightened person
to have had the insight to include handicapped citizens in
the performance.

The audience was staring at the handicapped actors.
In the early part of the first act, the stage was set. The
audience was introduced to the different characters, and
development of the story began. But when the magic
started to take over, all the actors became one body. The
body reached out into the audience, and they too, became
one with the work.

Now, what transpired to engage people to this level
of community enjoyment? First, of course, a gifted play-
wright with Mother's guidance wrote a great body of
work. Then many students and adults spent endless days
rehearsing the performance. Local artists were enlisted to
erect the set and create costumes for the actors. Pit musi-
cians introduced music to enhance scenes, strengthening
the actor's voices. The finishing touch was the audience,
now seated in this state of the art theatre.

Do you think one actor, isolated with one audience
member, could have achieved the level of entertainment
that this group was capable of? Are the health caregivers
in this country in the theatre at all, or are they in the park,
watching some kid street dance until he breaks his arm?

Caregivers, you can write prescriptions until your prescription pads melts down. Still you will lose the battle
of curing the street dancer's injuries. If you'd support a

program that encourages students to study street dancing as an art form, injuries would start to decrease. Teachers could introduce parameters of safety.

Bloodletting was the withdrawal of blood from a patient to cure or prevent illness and disease. Bloodletting was based on a system of medicine in which blood and other bodily fluid were regarded as "humors" that had to remain in proper balance to maintain health. It is claimed to have been the most common medical practice performed by surgeons from antiquity until the late 19th century, a span of almost 2,000 years. Bloodletting had some pretty fuzzy science associated with it. Doctors were being taught by Teachers to drain blood, not understanding the complete body. Does any of this sound familiar? We replaced bloodletting with science, which in my opinion limits the chance of curing diseases by being fragmented.

The trouble is that science is taught in a bubble, not balancing the education of human culture with advancements in medicine. Currently professionals have attitudes that science will cure man's problems with this isolated knowledge. Well, it will never happen without partnering with experts knowledgeable in the changing social norms in our society.

We presently have healthcare providers floating around in a sterile dinghy trying to rescue drowning patient's in a sewer. What would the Mother suggest they do? Teachers you'll have to clean up the sewer for the caregivers. The simple act of shunning smoking in public places saved far more people from lung cancer than all of the advanced sciences created by man to this date. Teachers you can save hundreds of students from lung cancer while the doctor is saving one. Of course, evil has found a way of reinventing itself by replacing tobacco with marijuana. Now, you have some more work to do, compliments of medical marijuana.

Do you ever wonder why you cannot see evil until its reinvents itself as a plague on mankind? It's because our candles are carried with cupped hands. We are afraid the wind will blow out our only source of light. If you placed all the candles under the Tree of Souls together and wrapped an idea around their base, a great torch would be created. Now, opening your hands to let the light flow outward, a path would appear for all of us to find our way. When the strong winds blow on a forest fire does it go out? No it becomes a firestorm, increasing in strength that goes out only when it consumes everything in its path.

My knowledge was limited by the people that I touched during my life's journey. I increased my understanding by drilling down into the soil as a worm would do, to discover the root system of the plant. For it's there, the truth you are seeking is found. Many plants have different root system, but the Mother's lessons are universal. When you are lost in the forest, let our Mother's teachings guide you to a place where the path becomes recognizable. Follow that path no matter how faint it is, because eventually you will be led to the Tree of Souls.

20

SENATOR JOHN MCCAIN

*"War is wretched beyond description, and only a fool
or a fraud could sentimentalize its cruel reality."*

T HANKS TO ALL THE MEDICAL STAFF THAT
served their country during the Vietnam War.
The wounded men who made it home alive owe you all
a big hug. The loved ones of the guys who didn't make it
home, can take comfort knowing that you did your best
to save them.

I'm dedicating my journal stories to the nurses that
were there for me in my hour of need. For without their
dedication to the nursing profession, I'm certain I would
not have come home from the war. If you hadn't been
there for your country, I would not have fathered my own
daughter who grew up to become a nurse herself. She
now continues to heal patients through the time-honored
profession of nursing.

I heard a wonderful story about the great fires in Yel-
lowstone National Park. Rangers doing an evaluation of
what damage the fires had done came upon a dead mother
quail sitting upright. On further inspection, they discovered she was on her nest. One of the rangers reached over,

lifting the mother off her nest, only to find live baby quail under her body. Rather than fly away to save herself, this mother gave her life to save the brood. Nurses who served in the Vietnam War, flew into the fires to save the brood at their own peril. Their professionalism remained steadfast, ready to serve our nation's wounded warriors during those difficult days.

Many of those nurses have fallen themselves, gone to be with the Lord. I wish I'd thanked them many years ago.

Mother said, "It's not too late. Remember my eighth gift: *Knowledge must have history associated with it to include information from beyond our short lifespan.* Remember, knowledge does not start at your birth or end and your death."

Wherever you great patriots are, thanks for saving me, I wrote this final story for all of you.

Julia Elizabeth Connor was my mother's maiden name. She was not a professional nurse, more like a natural healer of bodies and souls.

On a Sunday morning after church, Julia Elizabeth Connor decided to take a ride out to the old farmstead her parents left her. After a thirty-minute ride on bumpy farm roads, she pulled her rusty Ford F-150 pickup truck off the blacktop onto the dirt driveway. She switched the ignition key off. The truck hiccupped, sputtered, and finally the engine died.

Julia, now a retired nurse, climbed down from the running board, slamming the door behind her. She hasn't been to her parent's old farm since last fall. She walked to the old chestnut tree stump. A bead of sweat formed on her brow. She stopped to take inventory of what's changed since her last visit. The place always brought back so many memories of her childhood, the summer days she spent playing with her dolls on her momma's front porch.

She remembered her dog, Chip, that would chase his tail until he became dizzy. Chip was her constant companion as she was growing up. Wherever she went, he followed. When he was tired and ready for a nap, he'd allow her to play nurse, bandaging up a pretend injury.

Her daddy gave her the job of collecting eggs; he would carry her on his shoulders to the chicken coop. There, she'd reach under the old laying hens, being careful not to get pecked, and feel around for a warm egg. If she found one, daddy would say, "Eggs for breakfast in the morning."

On warm summer evenings, her momma would make homemade strawberry ice-cream. They'd all sit under the chestnut tree, eating at the pace of dripping ice-cream. Chip would sit staring at them, waiting for a drop of ice cream to hit the ground.

Chip died at 15 years old, and Julia's daddy buried him in back of the machine shed wrapped in a braided rug, which he always laid on just inside the back porch door.

Julia misses all of them and wiped tears from her eyes, laughing at herself for getting so emotional over times gone by. She thought, I guess the memories are why I keep this old place.

Over the years the wind had blown the wooden structures down, and once on the ground, they rotted quickly. She could just make out the fieldstone foundations that once anchored the buildings.

The once pastured lot was now overgrown with long prairie grasses. Purple violets had found a new home from the surrounding wood lot. She recalled the time she and her daddy planted the lilac bushes that bordered the farm-house wall. Her mother's favorite plant was the climbing red rose bush, planted just below the front room parlor.

She listened carefully, hearing the sounds of honey bees. "I wonder if they're working momma's old rose bush for nectar."

Carefully she worked her way down a stand of lilacs to see if the rose bush was still there. Pushing through the thick bushes, she was surprised to see that, yes indeed, the rose bush was there. The plant was in full bloom. Her momma would be pleased, she thought. She felt an unfa-miliar tightness in her chest, took a few full breaths, then sat down on the rock wall to rest.

After a few minutes of rest, it was as though the bush spoke to her, directing Julia to look at the flowers that were just coming into bud.

"See those buds that haven't shown their beauty yet? They represent the young nurses that will serve our nation in the future. Now, dear, shift your attention to the fully developed blooms. Their color, texture and fragrance are at their peak. They represent the nurses presently serving our nation.

"Finally, do you see the flowers that are nearing the end of their blooms? The petals are wrinkled and torn, and their color has darkened, losing some of their splendor. They represent you, Julia, and the nurses that have served our nation in the past."

Understanding the cycle of roses, it was obvious to her that those blooms were in the last days of their lives.

The rose bush said, "Do you see some have fallen to the ground beneath me?"

"Well, my eye sight isn't very good," Julia said, "but it

looks like spent blooms have fallen beneath the bush in a pattern that resembles old glory, our precious flag."

"Yes, you're right. Kneel and pick one up. Place it on the rock wall that you sit on."

She picked one up and placed it on the bleached-out rock wall, then recognized a name written on the spent bloom. It was the name of a soldier from the 9th Infantry Division. She had taken care of many soldiers from the 9th while serving in Vietnam. Using her hand she swept what was left of the blooms into a pile, and arranged them on the wall. They all had the names of the men who died in her care while she served in the Vietnam War.

Julia felt a refreshing wind starting to blow. It swirled every spent bloom on the rock wall into a wind tunnel of roses. Those rose petals were joined by buds and fully developed blooms from the bush. Yellow blooms appeared in the tunnel. The tunnel flattened out horizontally and was woven into the shape of a carpet, with red roses, green buds, and a yellow ribbon surrounding the border.

Julia rubbed her eyes to get a better view; the carpet was clearly in the shape of the 9th Infantry Division uniform shoulder patch. Eight 9th Infantry division soldiers stood at parade rest alongside the carpet.

She became frightened of what would come next, so she did what a child would do when threatened. She pulled both knees to her chest and covered her eyes with her hands. Her breath was labored; a tremor of pain ran down her arm.

Her parent's voices spoke. "Elizabeth, don't be afraid. We've sent these men to bring you home to us."

Her breath came back to a normal rhythm. The pain

left her arm, replaced by a peaceful comfort. Julia knew it was her parents, because they always called her Elizabeth when she was upset.

Julia asked her mother, "What is the meaning of the carpet?"

She replied, "It has been woven for you by the people that you have touched in your life as a nurse. Green is from the young nurses, red is from the nurses presently serving our nation and the deep burgundy is from the nurses that served with you."

"What about the beautiful yellow ribbon that borders the carpet?"

"Oh, that's from the Vietnamese you treated while serving in Vietnam."

Julia heard a dog bark in the background.

"Yes," her dad said, "that's Chip and he needs a bandage."

Julia stretched out her arms and the men of the 9th Infantry division assisted her onto their division patch made of roses.

The leader of the honor guard stepped to the front of the carpet, calling the men to attention. He presented her with the United States Flag while speaking these words:

"Julia Elizabeth Connor, we are eternally grateful for your service to us. It's been an honor to have served with you."

The men all saluted in unison, then came to their appointed positions on the border of the carpet. The carpet floated to a transport position. With the men of the 9th Infantry Division by Julia's side, they ascended to heaven.

Where have all the roses gone?
Long time passing
Where have all the roses gone?
Long time ago
Where have all the roses gone?
Picked by nurses every one
When will we ever learn?
When will we ever learn?

God bless the Nurse's Corp for their service to our Nation, and God Bless America.

9 781627 876162